CHARLES SPERONI, Professor of Italian at the University of California, Los Angeles, and a specialist in the study of the Italian Renaissance, is the author of numerous articles and monographs on Italian folklore, proverbs, and facetiae. He prepared the first English translation of all 495 extant letters of Michelangelo for Irving Stone's *The Agony and the Ecstasy* and *I, Michelangelo, Sculptor.* Professor Speroni is the founder of the Italian Department at the University of California, Los Angeles, President of the Dante Alighieri Society, and Associate Editor of the *Italian Quarterly.* He has been awarded the Star of Italian Solidarity and Head of Minerva, Silver Medal by the Italian government.

Wit and Wisdom of the Italian Renaissance

# WIT AND WISDOM OF THE ITALIAN RENAISSANCE

❧ ❧ ❧

*BY CHARLES SPERONI*

*University of California Press*
*Berkeley and Los Angeles*
1964

*University of California Press*
*Berkeley and Los Angeles, California*
*Cambridge University Press · London, England*

© 1964 BY THE REGENTS OF THE UNIVERSITY OF CALIFORNIA

*Library of Congress Catalog Card Number: 64-13475*
*Designed by Marion Skinner*
*Printed in the United States of America*

*To Carmela*

❦ *Therefore, whatever moves to laughter cheers the spirit and gives pleasure, and for the moment keeps one from thinking of those irksome troubles of which our life is full.* ❦

*Castiglione,* Book of the Courtier, *II, 45.*

# CONTENTS

# INTRODUCTION

WAS THE Renaissance an especially witty period? Was it a wise one? It is hazardous to state, and perhaps even more difficult to prove, that one period of high civilization was unmistakably wittier or wiser than another. There is no doubt, however, that the glorious time in Western civilization which we call the Renaissance witnessed an altogether unusual interest in witty anecdotes of all types, and in all sorts of apophthegms, maxims, proverbs, and proverbial phrases.

In that period, when artists and humanists alike looked back with awe and admiration to the ancient cultures of Greece and Rome, so keen was the desire to know everything those distant ancestors of ours had thought and said that not only their great works were rediscovered and restudied with a fervor unknown before, but also their minor ones, and among these their apophthegms and sayings. At one point the interest of Renaissance man in these latter grew so great that, not surprisingly, two of the most monumental collections of classical apophthegms and adages ever assembled were published between the end of the fifteenth and the beginning of the sixteenth centuries: Erasmus' *Apophthegmatum opus* and *Adagia*.

The apophthegm that flourished in Classical Antiquity was a brief narrative, often anecdotal, that usually extolled the deeds and the sayings of illustrious men —Socrates, Plato, Alexander the Great, and so on— but at times also those of lesser individuals; and the sayings, as they were generally wise, occasionally were also witty. If it is true that the apophthegm tended to instruct, it is also true that, according to the best didactic practice, it often chose to do so in an entertaining manner, and it did not hesitate to combine the useful with the agreeable. Although only few examples of Greek apophthegms have come down to us, there is ample evidence that they were very popular.

The apophthegm flourished also, and perhaps even more, among the Romans, who, judging by the fact that Cicero found the Greek apophthegms rather flat, had even a greater propensity for pungent witticism. Witty anecdotes and witticisms in general were held in high esteem by many ancient Romans: Plautus, whose comedies abound in witticisms; Caesar, who in his leisure gathered pleasantries and anecdotes; Plutarch, whose apophthegms met with great favor for many centuries; Aulus Gellius, who included many witty anecdotes in his *Attic Nights;* Macrobius, whose *Saturnalia* enclose a veritable collection of Roman pleasantries; and others. But by far the most important Roman work is Cicero's *De oratore,* which not only cites many witty anecdotes, but also makes a thorough analysis of wit and humor. This work was to exert a great influence on later writers.

The moralizing and even the witty anecdote were not forgotten during the Middle Ages; indeed, the moralizing anecdote—the "exemplum"—was highly cultivated in patristic literature. But, needless to say, in the works of the Church Fathers as well as on the lips of preachers who illustrated their sermons with all sorts of more or less pointed *exempla,* wisdom and morality were the lessons to be imparted, and wit and humor were only incidental. But wit and humor were at times an important ingredient to hold the interest and the attention of the listeners, and we have an excellent example of this as late as the first decades of the fifteenth century in the sermons of the colorful Italian friar Bernardino da Siena.

It was in the Renaissance, however, when a new, open-minded contact was reëstablished with the ancient classical literatures, that the witty anecdote, largely under the influence of the ancient apophthegm, entered a new phase and acquired an independent life. And it is interesting to note that this type of witty and often licentious anecdote, to which Cicero had given the name *facetia* (hence the Italian noun *facezia,* and the English adjective "facetious"), was once again given the same name—this time permanently—during the height of humanistic studies of Classical Antiquity. This was accomplished by one of the great Florentine humanists, Poggio Bracciolini, who gave the title *Liber facetiarum* ("Book of Pleasantries") to a vast collection of anecdotes that he compiled around the middle of the fifteenth century.

The facetia of the Renaissance is, in general, a brief narrative that varies in length from a few lines to one or even two pages. Its main purpose is to entertain and excite laughter by relating a humorous occurrence that often finds its conclusion in a pungent, well-timed repartee. Most frequently, the shorter the anecdote, the sharper the wit. Many of the facetiae of the Renaissance are associated with a witty individual, sometimes a court buffoon. Incidentally, the facetia, or as it may be called in English the "pleasantry," seems to thrive best in a highly developed culture, for a sophisticated mind sees the comical side of people, situations, and things.

Before Bracciolini's time, the humorous tale already existed in Italy. Witty tales made a grand entrance into Italian literature first with the *Novellino* or *Cento novelle antiche* ("One Hundred Old Tales"—thirteenth century), with Boccaccio's *Decameron* (middle of the fourteenth century), and with Franco Sacchetti's *Trecentonovelle* ("Three Hundred Tales"—end of the

fourteenth century). In the above collections we find
several tales that are definitely related to the facetiae.
In general, however, especially in the *Decameron,* but
also in Sacchetti and to a lesser degree in the *Novellino,*
we are faced with real novelle, which are too long, or
too artistically elaborated and articulated, or both, to
be considered facetiae. Just the same, it cannot be denied that some of Sacchetti's novelle in particular are
so rich in sparkling wit and lively dialogue, and in
lightning-quick repartees, that they come very close to
the general spirit of the true pleasantry, which is shorter
than the Sacchettian tale and aims straight at the burst
of humor that springs from the final, barbed repartee.

Whatever its antecedents, the modern facetia begins
to have its own history as a separate genre in the first
half of the fifteenth century, thanks mainly—if not entirely—to the collection of facetiae assembled by Poggio
Bracciolini. This great discoverer of ancient manuscripts, who had traveled in various parts of Europe
and had peered into the hearts of his contemporaries
as well as into those of the classical authors of whom
he was so fond, toward the end of his life decided to
write in Latin the stories and witticisms with which he
and his friends of the Roman Curia had entertained
one another during what was then the equivalent of
long afternoon coffee-breaks! This is what Poggio tells
us on the last page of his collection of pleasantries:

"Before closing the series of these little stories of
ours, it is my intention to mention also the locale where
the majority of them were told. This was our *Bugiale,*
a sort of workshop of lies, which was founded by the
secretaries in order that they might have an occasional
laugh. Since the days of Pope Martin [Martin V
(1419–1431)] we had the custom of choosing an out-
of-the-way place where we exchanged news, and where

we would talk of various things, both in earnest, and to distract our minds. Here, we spared no one, and we spoke evil of everything that vexed us. Often the Pope himself was the subject of our criticism, and for this reason many came to that place for fear of being the first ones harassed. . . . Now my friends are dead, and the *Bugiale* no longer exists, and through the fault of the times and of men, the good fashion of jests and conversation is disappearing."

This is what Bracciolini wrote at the conclusion of his book of 272 pleasantries that he titled simply *Facetiarum liber* ("Book of Pleasantries"). But he was wrong in his gloomy forecast that the taste for story-telling and wit was fast vanishing: his was just another nostalgic statement of an elderly man hankering for "the good old times." (He was seventy-two when he penned those words.) On the contrary, the taste for pleasantries was becoming more and more widespread, and for this two things were especially responsible: the much talked-about and circulated *Liber facetiarum* it-self, and the rising taste—of humanists and courtiers, in particular—for elegant and witty conversation, such as was later exemplified in *The Book of the Courtier* of Baldassare Castiglione and the *Civil Conversation* of Stefano Guazzo. What Bracciolini did not know was that his lively, witty, fairly bawdy collection of anec-dotes was to start a regular deluge of analogous col-lections, many of which would be more or less heavily indebted to his own. There is no doubt that, if Cicero invented the word facetia, it was Bracciolini who gave it a new, lasting life, and wide circulation. Because the *Liber facetiarum* aimed to amuse, like the more urbane collection of novelle of Boccaccio's *Decameron,* it was destined to be both censured for its licentiousness, and much imitated—simply because it made interesting reading and because it satisfied a universal need—the need to forget the chores and problems of daily existence and to break into a hearty, relaxing laugh.

Thus, it is not surprising to find that soon after Bracciolini's pleasantries became known, other collections were put together, more or less independently, by other writers. In the same century in which Bracciolini was writing, of special interest are the collections of the humanist from Ferrara, Lodovico Carbone (1435–1482); of the Tuscan cleric Arlotto Mainardi, known as Piovano ("The Priest") Arlotto (1396–1484); of the great Tuscan poet and humanist Angelo Poliziano (1454–1494); of the Florentine Niccolò dal Bùcine (1448–1532?); and of the Umbrian-Neapolitan humanist Giovanni Pontano (1426–1503). Although all the above authors will be given individual attention at the proper place in the text, there are two who deserve special notice: Piovano Arlotto and Giovanni Pontano.

The book of pleasantries of Arlotto Mainardi, known as *Motti e facezie del Piovano Arlotto* ("Witticisms and Pleasantries of Priest Arlotto"), has been through the centuries the most generally popular book of anecdotes in Italy. Like Bracciolini's collection, it became popular from the very moment it was known, and its popularity never died out. Also, contrary to all other large collections of Italian pleasantries, in which the characters are legion, in Arlotto's collection all the pleasantries revolve around the wise, witty, likeable, down-to-earth priest of the church of San Cresci at Maciuoli, a village not far from Florence.

Giovanni Pontano occupies a special place in the history of facetiae, and not alone of the fifteenth century; for, like Cicero's *De oratore,* from which he derived his inspiration, his *De sermone* discusses the nature of wit and quotes, in the process, several illustrative anecdotes. His work became well known among the men of letters of his and the following century, and exercised a particular influence on the better-known work of Baldassare Castiglione.

As it also happened with the Boccaccian short story, the facetia, which had thrived in the fifteenth century in Italy, reached its peak of popularity in the sixteenth century, when numerous collections were amassed and published, and when countless writers made a conspicuous point of including pleasantries in their works: from Castiglione to Giovanni della Casa and Stefano Guazzo, from Pietro Aretino to Anton Francesco Doni and Angelo Firenzuola, to mention only a few. By the end of the century, with the collections of Orazio Toscanella (*I motti, le facetie, argutie, burle, et altre piacevolezze,* "Witticisms, Pleasantries, Puns, Practical Jokes, and Other Humorous Jests," published in Venice, 1561), Poncino della Torre (*Piacevoli e ridicolose Facetie* . . . , "Entertaining and Merry Pleasantries . . . ," 1581), and Cristoforo Zabata (*Ristoro de' viandanti,* "Solace of Travelers," 1589), to mention the best known, the facetia had actually run its course; indeed, these works are of only passing interest, except for the specialist.

In the first half of the sixteenth century, a new impulse to the already popular facetia came from the publication of Desiderius Erasmus' *Apophthegmatum opus* (1531), and also from Heinrich Bebel's collection of pleasantries (1495), both largely diffused throughout Europe.

Among the numerous authors of the sixteenth century who were directly concerned with our genre, of special interest are the following: Baldassare Castiglione (1478–1529), Leonardo da Vinci (1452–1519), Ludovico Domenichi (1515–1564), and Ludovico Guicciardini (1521–1589). There are others, to be sure, but they do not fall within the scope of the present work. Not all the above made special collections of pleasantries. Leonardo da Vinci, for instance, made no systematic collection, but his keen, witty mind was truly attracted by apophthegmlike anecdotes, which abound in his voluminous writings.

The truly significant, systematic collector of the sixteenth century was Ludovico Domenichi, an indefatigable polygraph who wrote on many subjects. Domenichi became interested in pleasantries fairly early in his life, and in 1548 he published a collection of them with the title *Facezie e motti arguti di alcuni eccellentissimi ingegni et nobilissimi signori* ("Pleasantries and Witticisms of Certain Most Excellent Wits and Most Noble Gentlemen"). This collection, incidentally, contained many of the short, pungent anecdotes that had been written by the great Poliziano, although at the time of Domenichi it was not yet known that the protégé of Lorenzo de' Medici had written and amassed over four hundred pleasantries and proverbs. Domenichi reworked his own collection on two additional occasions, and in 1564, just before his death, he completed the third and final edition—*Facetie, motti et burle di diversi signori et persone private* ("Pleasantries, Witticisms and Practical Jokes of Several Gentlemen and Private Citizens")—which, although it excluded many of the anecdotes of the first edition, contained nearly one thousand items!

Needless to say, Domenichi dipped with a heavy hand in all directions, both at home and abroad: he did not hesitate, for instance, to translate many facetiae from the Latin work of Pontano and from the German collections of Bebel (*Opuscula bebeliana, sive Facetiae Bebelii,* second edition, 1504), and Nachtigall (*Joci et sales mire festivi,* 1524). But by Domenichi's time facetiae were common property; and besides, in the sixteenth century plagiarism was not considered a serious infraction of an author's rights. Further, had not the German collectors availed themselves of the Latin and Italian collections in their turn?

Domenichi's is not only by far the largest Italian collection of pleasantries, but also the most entertaining and the wittiest of the whole sixteenth century, both in Italy and in the rest of Europe. Both because of its variety and relative urbanity, and because of its polished literary style, Domenichi's book became very popular and was often reprinted, *in toto* and also in expurgated form. This had to be the case, for Domenichi had learned a great deal from his predecessors, in particular from Castiglione's *Cortegiano;* in fact, his style and sense of balance were a far cry from the rough-and-ready, although very idiomatic and colorful, everyday spoken language of Arlotto's collection.

The other work of the sixteenth century that is especially significant for a comprehension of the popularity of our genre during the Renaissance is Baldassare Castiglione's *Il Cortegiano* ("The Book of the Courtier"), first published in 1528, almost immediately translated into the important European languages, and since printed countless times in the original Italian and in translation. *The Book of the Courtier* is a living portrait of Renaissance Italian courtly life. Its first goal is, of course, to analyze the attributes that a "perfect courtier" must possess: but it is actually more than such a limited analysis, for it discusses also the attributes of the "perfect lady of the Court," and it includes a thorough discussion of Platonic love and of pleasantries and practical jokes. The perfect courtier described by Castiglione must be a nobleman who is not only skilled in the use of weapons, proficient in the arts of chivalry, courageous, elegant in social intercourse, and highly educated in letters and the arts, but he must also be politely entertaining and know how and when to tell

a witty anecdote or play a practical joke, and know
what kind of anecdotes to tell and which practical jokes
to play. Castiglione was not original in his discussion
of humor, any more than he was completely original in
certain other aspects of his *Cortegiano*: among other
sources, he made good use of Cicero's *De oratore*—
whose purpose it was to give an idea of the qualifications
of the perfect orator—and, to a lesser degree, of Pontano's *De sermone*.

Castiglione imitated Cicero both in the general idea
of his work and in several details, including the section
devoted to the treatment of facetiae. But the *Cortegiano*
is not merely an imitation: by Castiglione's time the
classics had been well assimilated, so that what we find
in him is a true product of the Italian Renaissance, and
the substance of his work was the fruit of his own experience, both bookish and of the contemporary world
he knew so well. Because of the universal influence of
*The Book of the Courtier* on the polite society of the
various Italian courts of the sixteenth century, and later
on other European courts (particularly on the Spanish
Court of Emperor Charles V and his successors, on the
English Court of Queen Elizabeth, and on the French
Court of the seventeenth century) ; because of the classical presentation of wit and the wise use of it, and because of the large number of "examples" given by Castiglione, I have decided to include in the present anthology almost the entire section of *The Book of the
Courtier* devoted to facetiae and *burle* ("practical
jokes").

The pleasantries and jests of the Renaissance have
time and again been labeled as immoral and licentious.
There is no doubt that in practically every book of
pleasantries a good number of them are free, and several are plainly bawdy. But this was not true of facetiae
exclusively: all one has to do is to read some of the

comedies and novelle of the time! We must agree with
the Italian critic Francesco de Sanctis who, in writing
on Pietro Aretino (the libertine author of the sixteenth century), said that "obscenity was a sauce much
sought after in Italy from Boccaccio on." It is not surprising, therefore, if in the period that followed the
Council of Trent (1545–1563), the editions of pleasantries—but not exclusively of pleasantries—show the
more or less heavy hand of the expurgator. But it
should be pointed out that obscenity—where it exists,
for most pleasantries are not bawdy—lies not so much
in the obscene image, as in the gross terms used in the
narration. The pleasantry, particularly in the fifteenth
century, lacks polish and elaboration; it is concrete, not
subtle, more improper than obscene. Further, the matter
of what is vulgar and what is not is a relative matter:
it must be borne in mind that what we consider vulgar
today was not necessarily considered so in the Renaissance, or in any other period of human history. The Renaissance was a period of great individuality, of great ex-
uberance in the newly discovered freedom of thought
and of expression, and the "new man" was not easily
shocked: he was more amoral than immoral. In the
light of what we consider immoral today, we would have
to expurgate and condemn not only the collections of
facetiae, but also the collections of novelle, most of the
Italian comedies of the sixteenth century, some of the
pastoral dramas, and much of the jocose poetry, to say
nothing of many sculptures and frescoes of the time.
But there is no denying that in our genre, many of the
pleasantries are bawdy by whatever standards we may
wish to judge them: so much so, that both Castiglione
in his *Cortegiano* and Giovanni della Casa in his *Galateo*
(the book of etiquette of the Italian sixteenth century)
sternly warned against indulgence in obscene anecdotes.
But if, when we speak of the pleasantries of centuries

gone by, it is difficult at times to judge of the relative immorality of a given pleasantry, it is even more difficult to judge today its sense of humor. There is little doubt that a collector of pleasantries did his best to include in his book what he thought were especially good, witty anecdotes that would invariably excite the laughter of the reader. And yet, we must confess that a fairly large number of anecdotes we find in most collections do not seem really humorous to us. Even in reading the sane pages of *The Book of the Courtier,* we are surprised at times to hear Castiglione tell the reader that a particular anecdote caused a great deal of hilarity.

Again, we are forced to conclude that the sense of humor of sixteenth-century Italy was not in complete tune with ours: and by ours I mean not only American humor, but also contemporary Italian humor. There is no doubt that what a given people consider humorous is often not thought to be so by another people; and further, that what was humorous in Renaissance Florence is not necessarily humorous today. Nevertheless much timeless comedy pervades the facetiae.

Beyond wit and morality, the facetia, like the novella of the fifteenth and sixteenth centuries, adds a new dimension to the overall, complex picture of the Italian Renaissance. Very often when one thinks of the Renaissance, one conjures up the great names of artists (Brunelleschi, Donatello, Botticelli, Leon Battista Alberti, Raphael, Cellini, Michelangelo), of great men of letters (Poliziano, Lorenzo de' Medici, Luigi Pulci, Niccolò Machiavelli, Baldassare Castiglione, and Ludovico Ariosto), of the great popes (Julius II, Nicholas V, Alexander VI, Leo X, Clement VII, and Paul III), of the great families (the Medici of Florence, the Este of Ferrara, the Gonzaga of Mantua, the Montefeltro and the Della Rovere of Urbino, the Visconti and the Sforza of Milan, the Doges of Venice, the Aragonese kings of

Naples)—and thus one places the whole period on a sort
of Olympus, surrounded by a halo if not by clouds. Yet,
the "makers" of the Renaissance were as much part of
the people as the humble artisans and craftsmen of the
back streets of Florence and Rome. The facetiae show
that in the Renaissance people from all walks of life
liked to laugh, even if they did not like to be laughed
at, and bring into focus their human frailties, their good
points and their bad. At the same time, the taste for
even the grossest stories on the part of the humanists
who recorded them and the patrons for whom they
were written clearly shows the contrast that existed
between the refined exterior of the culture and the low
ebb of the morality of the time. The facetiae show that
if, at times, these people were not too fastidious at what
they were laughing, and even leaned toward the cruel,
the vindictive, or even the sadistic, it was because they
were wholly human and not demigods.

Further, like some of the novelle of the time, the
facetiae give an excellent picture of some of the customs
of Renaissance Italy, such as religious ceremonies, festivities, nuptial practices, vows, incantations, and tra-
ditions, and also references to historical events.

Moreover, the facetious anecdotes are rich in character types and the human comedy of the Renaissance.
Here we find princes, popes, dukes, cardinals, the lower
clergy, artists, merchants, common people, sailors, servants, and peasants. In the facetiae (as in the novelle
and comedies of the age) peasants, women, and priests
seem to bear the brunt of the barbed anecdotes. That
was traditional, however, and in all probability the
satire was not as bitter as it might seem at first; and no
sacrilege was meant. The comical was the goal in all
instances; and, as in the medieval French fabliau and
in satiric literature, certain characters were deemed to
add to the sense of the comical when satirized. But the

pleasantry spared no one, and nothing was sacred to it. In a way, the fact that the Italians of the Renaissance were able to laugh at all classes of people and at all facets of daily life was an indication of the great individual freedom and of the broad-mindedness of the times.

Several of the jests are chauvinistic: we find Florentines slandering the Sienese, the Sienese backbiting the Florentines; Tuscans maligning the Venetians, and so on. Tuscans in general, and Florentines in particular, seem to dominate the scene, and that is because there were more of them who wrote or invented jests. Also, the Florentines and the Sienese have always been proverbially endowed with a good dosage of wit, and this was fully recognized by no lesser authorities than Pontano and Castiglione.

In the present anthology I have tried to select those anecdotes that, to me at least, seem not too remote from our sense of humor: many of them, and I hope the reader will agree with me, could easily have been written last week—allowances being made for a few changes, of course. Some I do not regard as being particularly funny, but I felt that the reader should not be cheated of a few of the platitudes that were repeated in the Piazza della Signoria of Lorenzo il Magnifico's time!

Also, I have purposely avoided the truly coarse pleasantries whose exclusive goal was obscenity; but I felt obliged to set prudishness aside and to give a representative sampling of what those distant ancestors of ours considered good reading fun.

As for the distribution, my general rule has been to include under each author those pleasantries that are usually associated with his name; however, it was beyond my scope to make a scholarly study of authorship. In a few instances, in order to give the reader a better version of a given anecdote, I have forgone my general rule, but only rarely. Further, in a representative anthology such as the present one, it was inevitable that the key collections of Bracciolini, Arlotto, Poliziano, and Domenichi should make the largest contribution: the first three because of their originality, and Domenichi's because of its sheer magnitude and also because of its great popularity through the centuries.

I have arranged the various authors according to the chronological order of their works, with one exception —Baldassare Castiglione. Castiglione belongs between Leonardo and Domenichi; however, since Castiglione offers us an excellent "treatise" on the place and use of pleasantries and practical jokes, I have decided to place him at the end—a place of meditation, after the rapid reading of many isolated anecdotes.

In translating from the various authors, I have tried as well as I could to retain much of the original flavor —as I did also not long ago in my translation of Michelangelo's letters. Just the same, a *traduttore* (translator) will always be a *traditore* (traitor), although it is true that there are as many degrees of treachery as there are translators!

# I
## Poggio Bracciolini
### 1380-1459

# POGGIO

POGGIO BRACCIOLINI, often called simply Poggio, was born at Terranuova d'Arezzo. He was a pupil of the Greek scholar Emmanuel Chrysoloras and was a friend of many humanists. He was apostolic secretary to eight successive popes and accompanied John XXIII to the Council of Constance in 1414. At one point he lost the favor of the Roman Curia, and he spent four years in England. Later he was again made apostolic secretary, and he was in Rome between 1443 and 1453, during the pontificate of Nicholas V, the founder of the Vatican Library. In 1452 he accepted the position of secretary and historian of the Florentine Republic. He died in Florence in 1459 and was buried in the church of Santa Croce, where many great Italians have since been buried.

Poggio was an indefatigable and fortunate discoverer of ancient manuscripts in the libraries and monasteries of Italy and other European countries. Among his great discoveries were Quintilian's *Institutiones oratoriae,* and Lucretius' *De rerum natura.*

Poggio wrote many works in Latin, among which was a *History of Florence.* His book of pleasantries, the *Liber facetiarum,* was also written in Latin: Poggio wanted to prove that the noble language of ancient Rome could also be used successfully in a minor genre, in telling stories and anecdotes of daily life.

Poggio wrote 272 pleasantries between 1438 and 1452. There is no doubt that these anecdotes spread among his friends and admirers even before they were published in 1470. They reveal the sharp, witty, satirical, and at times vindictive spirit of the author. For some unexplainable reason Poggio included a handful of stories about some extraordinary events that were reported to have taken place in his day. One of these strange anecdotes has been included in the present anthology.

Poggio's stories met with a *succès de scandale* everywhere. In an invective against a fellow humanist, Lorenzo Valla, Poggio boasted that his stories were known far and wide among all peoples of Europe who could read Latin—and we must not forget that this was before the invention of printing; they met with an even greater success after the *Liber facetiarum* could be printed, thanks to the recent invention of Gutenberg. Before the end of the sixteenth century Bracciolini's pleasantries had been printed several scores of times both in the original and in translation.

The scholar Poggio knew that he would be criticized for having devoted his attention to a brand-new, minor genre; and for that reason he wrote his own apology in a brief introduction to the *Liber facetiarum*. In it he says: "I think there will be many who will censure these stories, both as being of no account and unworthy of the seriousness of man, and because one would like to see in them a greater elegance and a more animated style. But if I reply to my critics that I have read that our ancestors, men of the greatest prudence and learning, took delight in jests, pleasantries, and anecdotes, and that they received praise rather than blame for this, I believe that I shall have done enough to win back their good opinion. Therefore, who will want to believe that I have done a base thing in imitating them in this—since I cannot in other things—and in giving to the cares of writing the time that others lose in society and in conversation, especially when this is not an indecorous work and may give some pleasure to the reader? Indeed, it is an honorable and necessary thing —for which philosophers received praise—to provide relief for the mind weighed down by troubles and thought, and to make it rejoice by means of some gay recreation. . . ." And he goes on, apologizing to the reader for having expressed himself in rather simple, unadorned style. Bracciolini was concerned for his style, not for his sharp tongue against the cloth, or for the bawdiness of many of his pleasantries!

Bracciolini's facetiae were translated in their entirety into English in 1888. Thirteen of his stories were included in William Caxton's edition (1484) of *The Fables of Aesop.*

## *The poor sailor from Gaeta*

ALMOST all the poor people of Gaeta live off the sea. One of them, the most wretched sea-faring man in the world, after wandering to many places in search of a livelihood, at the end of five years returned to his miserable home, where he had left his wife. As soon as he landed, he ran to see his wife, who, by that time, despairing ever to see her husband again, was living with another man. Once he was inside his house and saw that it had been enlarged, repaired and repainted, he asked his wife for the reason of that great transformation. His wife replied without hesitation that it was all due to the grace of God, who gives comfort to all men. "Let us bless the Lord, then," said her husband, "who has bestowed such great fortune on us!" Then he went upstairs and found in the bedroom a much more beautiful bed and elegant furniture than they could possibly afford. Upon his asking whence all that had come, his wife replied that they owed it all to the grace of God. Again he thanked the Lord for having been so generous toward them. Thus, his wife accounted for all the other novelties he discovered around the house in the same manner: they all came from the generosity of God. While the husband was standing around completely stunned and dazzled by such liberality, there came into the house a little boy who must have been between three and four years of age. As little children are wont to do, the little fellow ran straight into the arms of his mother. Immediately the husband asked his wife whose child he was, and she replied that he was his. When he expressed his amazement that she should have given him a son without his having participated in his conception, she replied once more that it was all due to the grace of God. Whereupon, unable to control his indignation over this excess of divine grace, the husband said: "I must certainly give thanks to the Lord, who has taken such a keen interest in my affairs!"

## 2

### *The doctor who cured the insane*

℘ SOME of us were talking about the vanity, not to say stupidity, of certain people who keep falcons and hunting dogs. At one point Paolo Fiorentino said: "There is no doubt that that insane fellow from Milan was completely right." Whereupon, complying with our request, he told us the following story.

Once there was a Milanese who treated the weak-minded and the insane. In his house he had a courtyard in which was a pond of dirty and stinking water. He tied the patients to a post, and he immersed them into the pond, some up to their knees, others up to their buttocks, and others even deeper, according to the degree of their insanity; and he kept them steeping in the water, on an empty stomach, until he thought they were cured. Once they brought him a man whom he immersed thigh-deep. At the end of two weeks this patient was normal again, and begged the doctor to lift him out of the pond. The doctor complied with his request, on condition that he remain within the courtyard, and after a few days of good behavior, allowed him to walk through the house, but with the understanding that he was not to go out into the street.

Once, while he was standing on the threshold of the house, he saw a young man on a horse coming in his direction with a hawk on his fist, and with two hunting dogs. Since he had lost memory of all he had done or seen before his illness, what he saw now seemed a novelty. When the young man was near him, he asked him: "Say, let me ask you a few questions. What is that thing you are riding, and what is it for?"

"It is a horse," the young man replied, "and I use it to go hunting."

"And what's that thing you have on your fist called, and what good is it?"

"It is a hawk that has been trained to hunt wild ducks and partridges."

And the madman: "And what are those things that follow you, and what are they for?"

"They are dogs that have been trained to flush game."

"That's fine, but what is the total value of the game you catch at the end of one year?"

"I don't really know, but probably no more than six ducats."

"And how much do you spend for your dogs, hawk and horse?"

"Fifty ducats."

Then, struck with the foolishness of the young horseman, he said: "Goodness! You'd better get away in a hurry before the doctor returns home, for if you fall into his hands, crazy as you are, he will cast you into the pond to cure you along with the others, and I am sure he will immerse you up to your neck."

### 3
### *The man who got up late*

BONACCIO de' Guasci, a cheerful young man, always got up late while we were in Constance;[1] and when his friends teased him for his laziness and asked him what on earth he was doing in bed, he would reply smiling: "I listen to the dispute of two contestants. In the morning, when I wake up, there are two female figures by my bed, Solicitude and Laziness. The former invites me to rise, to move about, not to spend the day in bed; the latter strongly urges me to lie still, because outside it is cold, whereas my bed is nice and warm; she tells me that the body needs rest, and that one cannot work all the time. Then Solicitude returns to the attack with new reasons, and since their debate lasts a long time, I, who am an impartial judge, do not take sides; I listen to the contestants, and I wait for them to reach an agreement. Thus, waiting for the dissension to be settled, I get up late."

## 4

### *How a woman deceived her husband*

A FRIEND of mine, called Peter, told me one day a charming story concerning the shrewdness of a certain woman. He said that he used to have intimate relations with the wife of a rather dense farmer who, in order to avoid his creditors, often spent the night in the fields. One evening, at dusk, while my friend was with this woman, her husband returned home unexpectedly. The woman immediately hid my friend under the bed, and sailed into her husband scolding him bitterly for having come back, thus running the risk of being caught and thrown in jail. "A little while ago," she said, "the police came to get you and take you to prison; they searched the whole house, but I told them that you usually spend the night away from home; and so they left, but they threatened that they would soon be back." The poor fellow, who was frightened to death, was anxious to clear out, but at that hour the city gates were locked up. His wife continued: "What do you intend to do, you crazy fool? If they lay their hands on you, your goose is cooked." And since, quaking in his boots, he asked for her advice, she, who was ready to spring the trap, said: "Climb up into the dovecot. You will spend the night there; I'll close the shutter from the outside, and I'll remove the ladder so that no one will suspect you are up there."

He took his wife's advice; and she, in order to keep him from getting out of the dovecot, locked the little door from the outside. Then she removed the ladder, and brought her lover out of his hiding place. The latter, pretending to be one of the policemen who supposedly had returned in large numbers, began shouting, and the woman began asking that he have mercy on her husband. This increased the terror of the poor wretch who was in hiding. When the shouting subsided, the two lovers went to bed and spent the night cheerfully. The husband was left alone with the pigeons and their droppings.

## 5

### *A woodcarver asks some peasants who had come to ask for a crucifix whether they wanted the Christ dead or alive*

A FEW villagers from Aiello, a mountain hamlet in the Apennines, were sent to Arezzo to purchase a wooden crucifix that was to be installed in the church. They went to a carver who sold holy images, and when he realized that he was dealing with unusually uncouth and ignorant men, in order to get a good laugh at their expense, after he heard what they wanted, he asked them whether they wanted the Christ dead or alive. They took their time to take counsel; they discussed the whole thing among themselves in low voices and they concluded that they preferred him alive, for, if their fellow townsmen did not like him that way, they could always kill him!

## 6
### *Giannozzo Visconti*

ONCE an acquaintance of Antonio Loschi,[2] who was a wise and jovial man, showed him a letter addressed to the Pope. Antonio Loschi told him to correct it and to revise a few passages. The other man brought it back to him the following day unchanged. Loschi looked it over and said to him: "You must have mistaken me for Giannozzo Visconti." Whereupon we asked him what he meant, and he said: "Giannozzo used to be our mayor of Vicenza. He was a very good man, but vulgar and thick of body and mind. He often called in his secretary and had him write letters to the old Duke of Milan. He dictated the salutation and the complimentary close himself; the secretary wrote the rest, and when the letter was finished, showed it to him. Giannozzo read it and invariably found it meaningless and poorly written. 'I do not like it as it stands,' he told him. 'Go and correct it.' The secretary returned presently with the very same letter, without having changed an iota, but saying that he had corrected it and recopied it. Then Giannozzo took it, as if to read it; he cast a glance upon it and said: 'Now the letter is fine. Seal it and mail it to the Duke.'"

## 7
### *Exhortation of a cardinal to the Pope's soldiers*

DURING the war that the Cardinal of Spain fought against the enemies of the Pope, when the two armies were facing each other at Agro Piceno, and the combat was about to begin, the Cardinal was urging his soldiers to fight. He assured them that those who fell would dine with God and the angels; and, in order that they die more happily, he promised them the remission of all their sins. Then, having made this exhortation, he withdrew far from the battlefield.

Whereupon, one of the soldiers asked him: "Why aren't you going with us to that dinner?"

He replied: "I am not accustomed to eating at this time: I am not hungry yet."

## 8

### *Of a priest who buried a little dog*

❧ THERE was in Tuscany a country priest who was very rich. Once a little dog that was very dear to him died, and he buried it in the cemetery. The Bishop, who was anxious to lay his hands on the priest's money, heard about this and summoned him, accusing him of a very grave crime. The priest, who knew the Bishop's mind, put fifty ducats in his pocket and went to see him. When he came before the Bishop, the latter reprimanded him bitterly for having buried the dog in the cemetery, and ordered that he be cast into jail.

"My Father," said the shrewd priest, "if you had known the intelligence of my little dog, now you wouldn't wonder at his having been interred where people are buried, for while he was alive and even at death's door he was much smarter than humans."

"What does that mean?" asked the Bishop.

"In the last few instants of his life," replied the priest, "he dictated his will, and being aware of your indigence, he left you these fifty ducats which I brought along."

Whereupon, the Bishop approved the will and the burial, took the money, and absolved the priest.

## 9

### *Of a monk who delivered a very short sermon*

ON the feast of St. Stephen, many people had flocked into one of our hill towns from numerous places. It was customary for a monk to deliver a public sermon. It was getting late, and as the priests were hungry, first one priest, then another, whispered into his ear to speak very briefly. He ascended the pulpit and said: "Brethren, last year I addressed you from this very place. I spoke of the sanctity of the life, and of the miracles of this Saint of ours, and I omitted nothing of what I had heard about him, or of what is written about him in the holy books; I am sure you remember all I said. Since that time, I haven't heard that he has done anything new; therefore, make the sign of the cross, and may the Lord bless you."

## 10

### *Elegant reply of Dante, Florentine poet*

DANTE ALIGHIERI, our Florentine poet, was for some time a guest in Verona of Can della Scala,[3] a most liberal prince. At his court, the latter kept another Can, a vulgar Florentine, who was impertinent, ignorant, and good for nothing except foolish jokes and silly jests that Can della Scala enjoyed so much that he showered him with gifts. Dante, who was a most learned man, as wise as he was modest, naturally held the courtier in scorn as a stupid fool.

One day this Florentine came up with this question:

"How is it that you, who are considered so wise and so learned, are poor and beggarly, while I, who am a fool and an ignoramus, am rich?"

Whereupon, Dante said to him: "When I find a lord who resembles me and has my likes, as you have found one of your kind, he will make me rich."

## II

### *Of a woman who insisted on calling her husband lousy*

ꙮ ONE day we were speaking of the obstinacy of women.

"A woman from our part of the country," said one of the group, "was always at cross-purposes with her husband; she contradicted whatever he said, jumped on him, and always clung pigheadedly to what she had said in order to have the last word. One day she had a violent argument with him and called him lousy. The husband, in order to make her take back the word, began kicking her, punching her, and beating her with a cane. The more he beat her, the more she continued calling him lousy. Tired, finally, of beating her, he tied her with a rope and lowered her into a well, threatening to drown her if she did not desist. But the woman continued to call him lousy even when the water was up to her throat. Then the husband, in order to keep her from talking, dropped her entirely into the well, hoping that the danger of death would cure her obstinacy. But she, who was no longer able to speak and on the verge of suffocation, finding it impossible to express herself with her voice, did it with her fingers, and raising her hands above the water, she joined her thumb-nails and, as long as she could, made the gesture of killing a louse.

## 12
### *Of a gambler who was put in jail*

IN Terranova dice players are punished in various ways. A man I know was caught gambling; sentence was passed on him, and he was taken to jail. When anyone would ask him why he had been locked in jail, he replied: "Our mayor had me cast in jail because I gambled my money. What on earth would he have done to me if I had gambled *his* money?"

## 13
### *Of a man who was looking for his wife who had drowned in a river*

ANOTHER man, whose wife had drowned in a river, was looking for her body and was walking upstream.

A man who saw him marvelled at this and advised him
to carry out his search downstream.

"I would never find her that way," said the husband,
"for when she was alive she had the mania of contra-
diction, and she was so intractable and contrary to the
ways of others that, even now that she is dead, she must
be floating against the flow of the stream!"


## 14
### Witticism of Lorenzo, a Roman priest

❧ THE day that Pope Eugenius [4] made the Roman
Angelotto a cardinal, a jolly priest of the city, named
Lorenzo, returned home quite happy. When his neighbors asked him what had ever happened that had made
him so cheerful and sprightly, Lorenzo answered:
"Things have taken a good turn. Now I have the highest hopes. Since idiots and fools are made cardinals, and
since Angelotto is crazier than I, I too will be elevated
to the holy purple." [5]


## 15
### Charming trick played by
### a witty man on Pope Boniface

❧ POPE BONIFACE IX [1389–1404] was a Neapolitan
of the Tomacelli family. Now, it so happens that certain pigs' livers that have been chopped and stuffed with
the fat of the same animal are generally called "tomacelli."

During the second year of his pontificate, Boniface
went to Perugia. He was accompanied by his brothers

and many other members of his family, who, as it happens out of greed for money and property, had gathered around him. When he made his entrance into the city, Boniface was followed by a retinue of important people, and among these, his brothers and other relatives. The curious onlookers were asking for the names of the people in the retinue, and invariably the replies would be: "That one is Andrea Tomacelli," "that one is Giovanni Tomacelli." Thus, the word "tomacelli" was frequently repeated. "Goodness," a witty spectator exclaimed at one point, "that pig's liver must have been huge indeed to furnish so many and such large 'tomacelli'!"

## 16

### Of a priest who preferred
### ten virgins to a married woman

A FRIAR who was not very discreet was preaching to the people of Tivoli. He thundered vehemently and at great length against adultery, which he censured as an abominable sin. Among other things, he said that it was such a grave sin, that he himself would rather have ten virgins than one married woman.

Many of the men there present were of the same opinion.

## 17

### Story of a mountebank told
### by the Cardinal of Bordeaux

BEFORE he was made pope, during the conclave and also after, Gregory XII [6] had promised to do many things for the schism that in his time was troubling the church.[7] For some time he kept his promises, and he even went so far as to say that, rather than fail in keeping his word, he would abdicate the papacy. But later he let power go to his head; he went back on his promises and pledges, and he did not carry out any of the things he had said he would do.

The Cardinal of Bordeaux,[8] an austere and wise man, was deeply grieved by all this, and one day he said to me: "He has behaved toward us like that mountebank did toward the people of Bologna when he promised them that he would fly." I begged him to tell me what he meant, and he said: "Not long ago there was in Bologna a mountebank who announced publicly that he would fly from a certain tower that is located at approximately one mile from the city. On the appointed day many people gathered in that place, and the mountebank made fools of them by making them wait in the sunshine and without food until almost evening. All were anxiously staring at the tower, waiting for the man to fly. Every time he showed himself at the top of the tower, and began flapping his wings as if he were about to jump off and start flying, loud applause rose from the crowd that stood watching with open mouths. After sunset, the mountebank turned his back to the people and showed them his behind. And so all those disillusioned, hungry, and bored people returned to the city.

"In the same manner," he concluded, "after so many promises, the Pope gratifies us by showing us his behind."

## 18

### Of an archer who wounded Ridolfo

SEVERAL men from Camerino one day were passing
their time practicing archery outside the city walls. A
clumsy fellow shot an arrow and inflicted a slight wound
on Prince Ridolfo,[9] who was watching from a distance.
The awkward archer was seized, and, believing that by
doing so they would win the Prince's favor, everyone
suggested an appropriate punishment for the offender.
One of them proposed that his hand be cut off, so that
he would no longer be able to shoot his bow. Ridolfo
intervened and ordered that the man be released, saying that such a sentence would have been effective only
if it had been carried out before he was hit.

## 19

### Of the Duke of Anjou, who
### showed Ridolfo a treasure

ONCE a group of learned people were talking about
the vanity of those who take great pains in seeking and
acquiring precious stones. One of them said: Ridolfo
from Camerino [10] was quite right when he was traveling
through the Kingdom of Naples and proved to the
Duke of Anjou how foolish he was in the matter of
jewels. One day, when Ridolfo had gone to visit the
Duke in his camp, the latter showed him a precious
treasure that consisted of diamonds, pearls, sapphires,
and other stones of similar value. After he had looked
at them, Ridolfo asked how much those stones were
worth and what good they were. The Duke replied that
they were very valuable, but that they were of no use.

Then Ridolfo said to him: "I will show you two stones that cost me ten florins and that give me an income of two hundred every year." And he led the Duke, who was quite stunned by this, to a mill he had built. There, he showed him two millstones, saying that as for utility and value, they had it all over his precious stones.

## 20

### Of a quack who cured fools

RECENTLY there lived in Florence a man who had no trade, but who was bold and sure of himself. Once he learned from a doctor the name and properties of certain pills, which were supposed to cure many illnesses. He decided to become a doctor on the sole merit of those pills; thus, he made a large number of them, left town, and began making the rounds of the hamlets and the farms, claiming that he was practicing medicine. He distributed those pills for all illnesses, and, as chance would have it, a few people regained their health. The renown of that fool had spread among other fools, and one day a man who had lost his donkey came to him to ask whether he had a medicine that would make him find his donkey. He said yes, and gave him six pills to take by mouth. The peasant swallowed the pills; and the next day, when he went out looking for his donkey, they took effect and he had to get off the road to relieve himself. He entered a thicket of reeds, where he found his donkey grazing. As a result, he praised to the sky both the knowledge of the doctor and the excellence of the pills.

21

## Jest of a Venetian who
## did not recognize his horse

᭜ A GROUP of learned men were discussing the dull-
ness and stupidity of some individuals. Antonio Loschi,[11]
who was a very jovial man, told the others that once,
on a journey from Rome to Vicenza, he was riding with
a Venetian who, as far as he could tell, had not ridden
a horse many times. They stopped at a hotel in Siena,
where many other horsemen had also stopped. The
next morning, when all were preparing to get on their
way, the Venetian was the only one who was standing at
the hotel door, doing nothing, as if dumbfounded.

Struck by his negligence and laziness, Loschi ad-
monished him that if he wanted to leave with him, he
should immediately mount his horse. Whereupon he
said: "Of course I want to go with you, but I can't tell
my horse from the others; for this reason I am waiting
for everybody to get on horseback; when only one horse
is left in the stable, I will know that that is mine."

22

## Of a doctor and an ignoramus

᭜ ONCE Pope Martin [V, 1414–1431] was with his
secretaries, and they were talking about amusing things.
At one point the Pope narrated that in Bologna there
was a doctor who annoyed the legate with so much insistence that the latter told him he was crazy. At which
the doctor said: "When did you discover that I was
crazy?" "In this instant," said the legate. "You are
wrong," replied the other. "I was crazy when I made

you a doctor of civil law, since you are perfectly ignorant of it."

## 23
### *Witty reply of a Roman*

❧ ANOTHER secretary, I believe it was the Bishop of Aletto, related the witty remark of a Roman. A Neapolitan cardinal,[12] who was a silly and ignorant man, one day was returning from a visit to the Pope. He ran into a Roman citizen, who noticed that he was constantly smiling, as was his habit. The citizen asked a friend of his why that cardinal was smiling, and when he told him that he did not know, the Roman said: "Undoubtedly he is laughing at the Holy Father who made him a cardinal."

## 24
### *Of an old man who was*
### *carrying a donkey on his back*

❧ ONE day, among the secretaries of the Pope, it was asserted that those who yield to public opinion are subjected to the most abject slavery, because it is impossible to please everybody. To illustrate this point, one of those present told the following story, which he asserted to have seen written and illustrated pictorially in Germany.

He said that there was an old man who was walking with his son, who was still a boy, behind a donkey that they were thinking of selling at the fair. Along the way, some peasants who were working in the fields reprimanded the old man because he was letting the donkey go unloaded, instead of mounting it with his boy; after all, one of them was of advanced age, and the other was a young child, and they had no business wearing themselves out. Then the old man put his boy on the donkey, and he continued his journey on foot. Some other people saw them and censured the stupidity of the old man, who had set his hale son on the donkey, and he, who was feeble with age, followed on foot.

Having changed his mind, he had his boy dismount, and he got on the donkey himself. After they had gone a short distance, he heard others who were blaming him because he, who was the father, rode the donkey, and dragged his son behind like a servant, with no regard for his young age.

Believing that those people were right, the father had his boy get on the donkey with him, and thus they proceeded on their way. After they had gone some distance, a man asked him whether the donkey was his, and when he said that it was, the other scolded him for having no more consideration for it than if it belonged to someone else; he told him that the weight was excessive, and that one person would be enough for the donkey to carry.

After hearing so many and different opinions, the old man lost control of himself: he tied the hoofs of the donkey together, put a stick through them, and by resting it on his and his boy's shoulders, began carrying the donkey to the fair. But since this odd sight made everybody burst out laughing, the father threw the donkey into a nearby river and returned home. Thus he did not please anyone and lost a donkey into the bargain.

## 25
### *Shrewdness of a doctor*
### *when he visited his patients*

AN ignorant but shrewd doctor used to call on his patients with a disciple of his. As doctors are wont to do, he would feel the patient's pulse, and if he realized that he was faced with something more serious than usual, he laid the blame on the patient, saying that he had eaten a fig, or an apple, or something else that he had prohibited. Since his patients often confessed it, he was considered an omniscient man who was able to find out even the deception of the sick. His disciple was repeatedly struck by this, and once he asked the doctor how he learned such things: was it from the pulse, from ausculation, or from some loftier science? And the doctor, in order to reward him for the confidence he had in him, revealed his secret: "When I enter the patient's room," he said, "I look around warily, to see whether on the floor there is the residue of a fruit or of something else, such as the skin of a fig or the peel of a chestnut, the shell of a nut, the rind of an apple, or anything else. If I find some residue, I suspect that the patient has eaten a certain thing, and thus, if the illness has taken a turn for the worse, I blame the incontinence of the patient, and should something happen, I am no longer responsible."

Some time later, the disciple began to practice medicine himself, and he often had recourse to the same rebukes, saying that the patients had not followed his orders, and that they had eaten this thing or that, depending on the evidence he could spot. Once he visited a poor peasant: he administered a certain potion and told him that if he followed his orders he would soon be well. On the next day, when he called on him, he found that his patient was worse. That foolish and ignorant man, unable to guess the cause, began looking around but couldn't find any residues. He was at his wit's end, when he detected a donkey's packsaddle under the bed. He immediately began shouting that the patient had overindulged, and that he was amazed he wasn't already dead. Believing that the packsaddle was the residue of the roasted donkey, just as bones are the residue of meat, he pronounced that the patient had eaten a whole donkey.

## 26

### Of one who wanted to spend one thousand florins to become known

A fatuous young Florentine told a friend that he wanted to take long journeys, and that he wanted to spend one thousand florins to become known. His friend, who knew him well, said to him: "You would be wiser if you spent two thousand florins to remain unknown."

## 27

### A pleasantry of the celebrated Dante

WHILE our Florentine poet Dante was an exile in Siena, one day he was in the church of the Minor Friars absorbed in thought, with an elbow resting on an altar. A certain man came up to him and asked him a stupid question.

"Tell me," Dante said to him, "what is the greatest of all the beasts?"

"The elephant," replied the other.

"Very well, then," retorted Dante, "leave me alone,

you elephant, for I have more important things than your words to think about, and don't annoy me anymore."

## 28

*Jocose answer given by a woman to a man who asked whether his wife could give birth to a twelve-months child*

℘ A FLORENTINE who had been out of town for a year returned home and found that his wife was about to have a child. He couldn't quite resign himself to this state of affairs, and he was afraid that his wife had not been faithful to him. Since he feared that this had actually been the case, he went to seek the advice of a wise woman who lived in his neighborhood, and asked her if it was possible for him to become the father of a twelve-months child. Realizing that the man was an absolute fool, the woman tried to tranquilize him and replied: "It certainly is possible; for, if on the day that your wife conceived, she happened to see an ass, she will give birth to her child after one year, as those animals regularly do."

## 29

*Of a Florentine priest who went to Hungary*

℘ IN THE KINGDOM of Hungary there is the custom whereby, after Mass, the faithful who are having eye trouble go up to the altar, and they let the priest sprinkle their eyes with holy water from the chalice. At the same time, the priest pronounces several words from the holy books and asks for the relief of the afflicted ones.

Once a Florentine priest went to Hungary with Filippo, who was called "the Spaniard." On one occasion, after he had said Mass in the presence of King Sigismund,[13] he saw several people with severely blood-shot eyes come near him to have their eyes sprinkled with water from the chalice. Believing that their trouble was due to revelry, he took the chalice, as he had seen others do, and sprinkled them, saying in Italian: "Andatevene, che siate morti a ghiado" ["Get out of here, and drop dead!"] The Emperor-King heard those words, and couldn't refrain from bursting into laughter. The next day, at table, he repeated, in jest, the words of the priest, which made everybody laugh, except those afflicted with eye trouble, who got very angry.

## 30
### Of a highlander who wanted to marry a girl

A HIGHLANDER from Pergola [14] wanted to marry the young daughter of a neighbor. When he first met her, he felt that she was still too young and innocent, but her father, who was truly a foolish man, said to him: "She is more mature than you think; she has already had three children by the cleric of our parish priest."

## 31
### Of a peasant who hid a fox
### that was being pursued by dogs

A FOX that was being pursued by dogs during a hunt ran into a peasant who was threshing grain, and begged him to shelter him, and swore that, in return, he would never again harm his chickens. The peasant consented and hid the fox under a pitchforkful of straw.

A little later the hunters arrived on the threshing-floor, and asked the peasant whether he had seen a fox, and in what direction it had gone. He told them in so many words that the fox had gone in a certain direction, but with his eyes and his hand he kept pointing to the pile of straw. The hunters paid more attention to his words than to his gestures, and continued on their way.

Then, the peasant uncovered the fox and said to him: "Don't fail to keep your promise, for you owe your life to my words, since I told them that you were far from here."

But the fox, which had experienced great terror, and had seen the peasant's gesticulations, said: "Your words were good, but your gestures were wicked!"

## 32
### Of certain wonders related to Pope Eugenius

THIS year, when the Pontiff [15] came to Florence during the month of October, there was a lot of talking about many extraordinary occurrences, and they were related by such trustworthy individuals that it would be foolish to doubt their veracity.

Letters written from the town of Como by most reputable people who saw the whole thing relate that in a certain place, five miles away from there, a large number of dogs were seen at nine o'clock in the evening. There were, it was estimated, about four thousand of them, reddish in hue, and they were going in the direction of Germany. This first pack was followed by a large number of oxen and sheep; these were followed by foot soldiers and horsemen divided into companies and troops; many carried a shield, and there were so many of them that it looked like an army. Many of them seemed to have heads, others appeared headless. The last squadron was led by a man who was as tall as a giant; he was seated on an enormous horse, and was accompanied by a large number of beasts of burden of all kinds. This procession lasted almost three hours, and it was seen from various places. There are many witnesses of this, both men and women, who, in order to see better, tried to get close to it. After sunset, as if they had moved to other lands, the apparitions were no longer seen.

## 33
### How Petrillo cleared a
### hospital of all its riffraff

℧ THE CARDINAL of Bari, who was a Neapolitan, owned a hospital in Vercelli, a town in the Po Valley, and he derived little profit from it because of all the money he had to spend on the poor. In order to get more money from his hospital, he sent there one of his men, whose name was Petrillo.

When Petrillo found that the hospital was full of sick people and loafers who drained all the income of the place, he put on a doctor's smock and began examining all kinds of diseases in the various wards. Then he said to the inmates: "There is no medicine that can cure your sores, except an ointment made from human fat. Today, therefore, we shall draw lots, and we shall determine which one of you will have to be placed in a pot of water and boiled alive."

Frightened by those words, they all fled.

## 34
### The pleasantest sound

℧ ONCE, in the days of Boniface IX, a group of people were discussing which is the sweetest and most cheerful sound. Some suggested one sound, others another, until Lito from Imola, formerly a secretary to the Cardinal of Florence, and then a cardinal himself, said that the sound of the dinnerbell was by far the most cheerful for the hungry. Indeed, it is customary with cardinals to have the members of their household called to lunch and dinner by the sound of a bell, which often rings much later than certain gourmands would like, and which is quite welcome to the ears of a hungry person.

## 35
### Of the son of a prince who was
### ordered by his father to remain silent

℧ ONCE a Spanish prince had a slanderous and scandalmongering son, who had gained for himself the hatred of everybody. For this reason, his father had ordered him never to say a word, and he obeyed him. One day it so happened that both went to a solemn banquet given by the King. The Queen was also present, and she noted that the youth waited on his father hand and foot, and behaved as if he were deaf and dumb. The Queen, who was not an honorable woman, thought that he was really deaf and dumb, and trusting that he would be useful to her, she asked his father to let her take him into her service. Thus, she had him wait on her on all the most intimate occasions, and he often witnessed her debauchery.

Two years later another banquet was held, and, in the meantime, the King had often run into the youth whom everybody thought to be dumb. While he was serving the Queen, the King asked his father whether his son was dumb because of an accident, or whether he had been born that way. The father replied that he wasn't dumb at all, but that he had remained silent all along because he had ordered him to do so on account of his slanderous tongue. The King urged him to give his son permission to talk. The father hesitated for a long time, saying that only evil would come from it, but in the end, being solicited by the King, he ordered his son to speak. Immediately, the latter turned to the King and said: "Your wife is of such a nature that no whore is more wanton or more shameless than she." The King was stunned, and commanded him to hold his tongue.

## 36

### *Of a fat horseman*

A CORPULENT horseman arrived at Perugia. Many people were walking toward him, and since the inhabitants of that city are naturally witty, they began to make sport of him and they asked him why, against all conventions, he carried his baggage in front. And the horseman wittily replied: "I carry it in front because it is the only safe thing to do in a city of thieves such as this one."

## 37
### *Witty saying of a doctor*
### *who prescribed medicine at random*

℘ IT is customary in Rome for sick people to send a specimen of their urine to the doctor in order that he may diagnose and cure their illnesses.

Every evening a physician with whom I was personally acquainted wrote down on as many pieces of paper various prescriptions for all kinds of illnesses; then he put them all together in a bag, and the next morning, when specimens were brought to him, he reached into the sack, took out the first piece of paper he grasped, and as he gave it to a patient, he said: "Pray God that he gives you a good one!"

## 38
### *Advice to a man who was concerned*
### *over his debts*

℘ A MAN from Perugia was walking down a street with a sad and worried look on his face. He ran into a fellow who asked him what the matter was. He replied that he had a lot of debts and that he couldn't possibly meet the payments. "You blockhead," said the other, "mind your own business and let your creditors worry."

## 39
### Of a man who vowed a candle
### to the Virgin Mary

WHEN I was in England [16] I heard about the witty reply of a man who was the captain of an Irish merchant ship.

Once he was on the high seas and his ship was so badly tossed and buffeted by a storm that he despaired of bringing it safely into port. The captain made a vow that, if his ship were saved from the storm, he would bring a candle as big as the mainmast of his ship to a certain image of Our Lady, which was famous for granting such miracles. When a friend of his, who was on board, told him that he couldn't possibly keep his vow, for in all of England there wasn't enough wax to make such a large candle, the captain said to him: "Keep quiet, and let me promise what I like to the Mother of God, for when we are saved, she will be satisfied with a penny candle!"

## 40
### Of a widow who wanted an elderly husband

A WIDOW was confiding to a neighbor of hers that, although she no longer cared for the things of the world, she would nevertheless like to marry a peace-loving, elderly man. This was her desire, she said, more for the sake of companionship and mutual assistance, than for any other reason; for she was more concerned about the salvation of her soul than the frivolities of the flesh.

Her friend promised that she would find the right

man for her. The next day she went to see the widow, and she told her that she had found him; and that he possessed all the good qualities she desired, especially the one she really preferred: namely, that he lacked what other men have.

Whereupon the widow replied: "This man won't do at all; I wish to live in harmony with my husband, and if he doesn't have the peacemaker (that's how she called it), who will act as a middleman when, as it sometimes happens, we need someone to bring peace between us after a quarrel?"

## 41
### *Witty reply of a boy to Cardinal Angelotto*

THE Roman Cardinal Angelotto,[17] who was endowed with a biting wit, had a propensity for sarcasm, but little self-control.

When Pope Eugenius was in Florence, there came to see him an alert ten-year-old boy, who addressed him with few but wise words. Stunned by the seriousness of the boy and by the elegance of his speech, Angelotto asked him many questions, and he answered all of them with alertness.

At one point the Cardinal turned to those present and said: "Children, such as this one, who are talented and learned at a young age, when they grow older become dull-witted; and by the time they are old, they turn stupid."

Whereupon, the boy, without losing his composure, said: "There is no doubt that when you were a boy, you must have been the wisest of all."

## 42

### Of a Spanish bishop who
### ate partridges instead of fish

A SPANISH bishop, who was traveling on a Friday, stopped at an inn and sent the waiter to buy some fish. Since no fish was to be found, the waiter bought two partridges, and the Bishop asked him to cook them and to serve them to him for lunch. The waiter, who had bought them to be cooked on Sunday, was quite stunned by the request, and as he served them to the bishop, he reminded him that on Friday it is forbidden to eat meat. Whereupon, the Bishop said to him: "I eat them as if they *were* fish." But since the waiter seemed baffled by his reply, he added: "Don't you realize that I am a priest? Which do you think is a greater miracle, to change bread into the body of Christ or partridges into fish?" Then he made the sign of the cross, commanded that the partridges be changed into fish, and ate them as such.

## 43

### Of a fool who said that
### the Archbishop of Cologne was a quadruped

THE Archbishop of Cologne, who is now dead, was very fond of a simpleton; and he often had him sleep in his own bed. Once there was also a woman in the same bed; and the simpleton, who was at the foot of the bed, felt that there were more feet than usual. He touched one foot and asked whose it was. Then he touched a second foot, then a third, and then the fourth. Every time the simpleton asked, the Archbishop an-

swered that it was his foot. Then the fool jumped out
of bed, ran to the window and began shouting at the
top of his voice: "Hurry, everybody! Come and see a
new and extraordinary prodigy. Our Archbishop has
become four-footed!"

## 44
### How a daughter excused her sterility
### to her father

AFTER several years of marriage, a rich man sent
his wife back to her family because she was sterile.
Her father took her aside and asked her why she hadn't
done all she could in order to have a child, if necessary
even by having extramarital relations. The daughter
replied: "Dear father, it's not at all my fault; because,
in order to get pregnant, I availed myself of all the men-
servants in the house, and even of the stablemen, but it
was all for nothing."

## 45
### Of a preacher who said five
### hundred instead of five thousand

A PRIEST was giving his flock a sermon on the Gospel, and he mentioned how with five loaves of bread our
Savior fed five thousand people; but instead of saying
five thousand, he said five hundred. The altar boy told
him that he had made a mistake, because the Gospel
says five thousand. Whereupon, the priest said to him:
"Be quiet, you fool! They will have a hard time believing five hundred."

## 46
### *The shouting preacher*

A MONK who often preached to his parishioners had the foolish habit of shouting at the top of his voice. As he preached, a woman wept so noisily that her sobs sounded like roars. The monk noticed this; and, believing that the woman was moved by his eloquence, by the love of God, and by her conscience, called her and asked her for the reason of her lamentations. He told her that if she had been shaken by his words, she should by all means weep, for that was a pious act.

The woman answered that she was grieved and moved because of his shouting and ranting. She said that she was a widow and that her poor husband had left her a donkey, thanks to which she had been able to live from hand to mouth. Her donkey used to bray day and night just as loudly as the monk did; but the donkey had died and left her starving. She told the preacher that when she heard his loud screams, she thought of her donkey and could not help crying.

## 47
### *Of a young woman who was mocked*
### *by her old husband*

A FLORENTINE who had already reached old age married a young woman who had been instructed by her married girl friends not to yield the fortress to her husband's first attacks on her wedding night. She followed their advice; and her husband, who was ready to set sail on the sea of love, asked her why she wasn't more tract-

able with him. The coy virgin said that it was the fault of
a headache she had; and the man, dropping the sails,
turned his back to her and slept until dawn.

When the girl saw that her husband no longer sought
her, she grieved over the advice she had been given,
woke up her husband, and told him that her head no
longer ached. And he replied: "Now my tail aches,"
and he left his wife a virgin.

## 48

### The unlocking of Cardinal Angelotto's mouth

ANGELOTTO, a Roman, was an inveterate gossip
whose caustic tongue spared no one. When, through the
fault of the times in which he lived, not to say through
the stupidity of men, he was made cardinal, one day,
as is customary in the secret Consistory of Cardinals,
he was bound to silence. It is commonly said that the
newly elected cardinals keep their mouths locked until
the Pope opens them by granting them permission to
speak. One day I asked the Cardinal of Saint Marcellus
what they had decreed in the Consistory, and he replied: "We have unlocked Angelotto's mouth."

"That's too bad," I replied, "it would have been
better to lock it with a heavy padlock." [18]

## 49

### How Ridolfo lent a good horse

ONCE a nobleman from Piacenza asked Ridolfo
from Camerino [19] for a horse that should have so many
good qualities and be of such great beauty as to sur-
pass all the horses in the Prince's stables.

In order to comply with his request, Ridolfo sent

him a mare and a stallion of his, with the advice that
he was sending along those implements to enable him
to make a horse to suit himself, for he did not have the
horse he had requested.

## 50
### *Of an English dyer who had an extraordinary adventure with his wife*

WHEN I was in England,[20] a dyer had a ludicrous
adventure that deserves being recorded here. This man
was married and in his household had many servants,
among whom was one maid he especially coveted because she seemed to him more attractive than the others.
Many times he asked her to go to his room; and she
told this to her mistress, who advised her to consent.

When the day and the time which had been set for
the appointment came, instead of the maid, the mistress went to the dark and secret meeting place; the
man came and, unaware that the woman was his wife,
achieved his goal.

When he was through, he left and told one of his
apprentices what he had done and suggested that, if he
wished, he too could take the girl. The apprentice went;
and since the wife thought he was her husband, she
received him without saying a word. Then a second apprentice came; and the woman, in the firm belief that he
too was her husband, submitted to the sacrifice for the
third time.

When it was finally possible for her to get out, the
woman slipped secretly out of the small room; and,
that night, she rebuked her husband for being so cold
with her and so passionate with the maid as to visit
her three times in one day.

The husband pretended not to know anything of his

blunder, nor of his wife's sin, of which he had been the cause.

## 51

### *Subtle remark of a Florentine on the children of the Genoese*

ᴈ FRANCESCO QUARENTA, a Florentine merchant, lived in Genoa with his wife and his family. His children were skinny and frail; the children of the Genoese, instead, were husky and strong.

Once a Genoese asked Francesco for an explanation of why his children were so stunted and thin, while theirs were all the opposite. And he replied: "It's very simple. I beget my children alone, whereas you Genoese beget your children with the help of many other men."

It is known that the Genoese no sooner get married than they go to sea to trade, leaving their wives behind—as they are wont to say—in the care of others.

## 52

### *Biting answer to a merchant who spoke ill of others*

ᴈ CARLO GERIO, a Florentine merchant, was one of those bankers who follow the Roman Curia. As is customary with those merchants who carry out their business in various parts of the world, he once went to Avignon; and later he returned to Rome. There, he was having supper one evening with some friends; and he was asked how the Florentines fared who were in Avignon. He replied that they were happy, and as crazy as foxes, because, he added, if one lives in that city a whole year, he goes mad.

Then one of the guests, named Allighieri, who had a biting wit, asked Carlo how long he had been in Avignon; and he replied that he had lived there only six months. Whereupon Allighieri said to him: "You must be a man of great talent, Carlo, since in barely six months you have accomplished what it takes others a whole year!"

## 53
### Witty saying of a man who had promised to educate a donkey

A COUNTRY squire wanted to seize the property of a vassal of his who constantly boasted of knowing how to do many things. In order to carry out his purpose, he asked him, under a severe penalty, to teach a donkey how to read. The man replied that this was impossible to do, unless he was granted a long time to teach the donkey to do something. Since the country squire allowed him to ask for all the time he wished, he asked for ten years.

Everybody made fun of him because he had taken upon himself an impossible task, but he comforted his friends in this fashion: "I am not afraid of anything, because during that time either I will die, or the donkey will die, or my lord will die."

## 54
### Crocodile tears

A MAN took some birds out of a cage and killed them by crushing their heads. While he was doing this, it so happened that tears began flowing from his eyes. Then one of the birds in the cage said to the others:

"Take heart. I see that now he is weeping, and I am sure he will have mercy on us."

The oldest bird replied: "My son, do not look at his eyes, look at his hands."

## 55
### *Of a man who wore several chains around his neck*

A CONCEITED Milanese soldier, born of a noble line, came as an ambassador to Florence; and every day, out of ostentation, he wore various types of chains around his neck. Niccolò Niccoli,[21] a most learned and caustic man, noticed his stupid vanity and said: "Other madmen bear to be tied with one chain, but he is such a madman that he is not satisfied with one."

## 56
### *Ridolfo, Lord of Camerino, and the ambassador who abused the Signori*

DURING the war between Pope Gregory XI [22] and the Florentines, the province of Piceno and most of the Roman provinces deserted the papal cause. The ambassador of Recanati [23] was sent to Florence to thank the Priors for the liberty which the people of his city were enjoying thanks to the help of the Florentines. When he came to Florence, he spoke abusive words against the Pope and his ministers, and particularly against all lords and tyrants, taunting their bad government and their crimes, without the slightest respect even for Ridolfo, who was then the leader of the Florentine army and was present at the hearings of the ambassadors and was listening to the lengthy invective against himself.

At the conclusion, Ridolfo asked the ambassador to what department or profession he belonged, and the ambassador replied that he was a doctor of civil law. Whereupon Ridolfo asked him how many years he had studied law. When he replied that he had devoted over ten years to the study of law, Ridolfo exclaimed: "How I wish you had devoted a single year to the study of discretion!"

## 57

### Extraordinary evenness
### between penitent and confessor

A CERTAIN man, either in earnest or to make sport of a priest, went to him saying that he wanted to confess his sins. Upon being asked to recite the sins he recalled having committed, he said that he had stolen something or other from a man, but that the latter had stolen even more from him. And the priest said: "One thing counterbalances the other, and you are even."

Then the man added that he had beaten a fellow with a stick, but that he too had been dealt a few blows in return. In the same fashion, the priest said that the punishment counterbalanced the guilt. The man recited other similar sins and the priest told him every time that one thing cancelled the other.

At one point the penitent said: "Now I have one sin left, which makes me blush and feel great shame, especially in your presence since in this case you are the offended party." As the priest encouraged him to take heart and to say frankly what he had done, after holding out for a while, and being prodded by the concern of the priest, he said: "I have had your sister."

"And I," said the priest, "have had your mother several times, and as was the case with the other sins, one thing balances the other."

For this equivalence of sins, he absolved him.

## 58

### *Of the man who was being taken to be buried, and spoke*

THERE lived in Florence a simpleton called Nigniaca, who was not irascible, but rather genial.

Several jolly young men, who wanted to laugh at his expense, decided to make him believe that he was seriously ill. After they had planned the whole thing, upon leaving the house one morning one of them ran into him and asked him what was the matter with him, for his face was pale and troubled. "Nothing is the matter with me," he replied.

Later, after he had gone a certain distance, another member of the clique asked him whether he was running a temperature, for so it seemed, judging by his wan and drawn face. The simpleton began wondering whether they weren't speaking the truth after all. He was proceeding slowly and hesitatingly when he met a third man who, as had been agreed, said as soon as he saw him: "Your face clearly indicates that you are very sick and that you have a very high fever."

The poor fellow became more and more concerned; he stopped and began wondering whether he was really running a temperature. A fourth person came up to him and told him that he most certainly was ill; he said that he was surprised he was not in bed, and persuaded him to go straight home; he offered him his friendly assistance, and promised that he would take care of him like a brother.

The fool turned back, as if seized by a sudden illness, and put himself to bed as if he were at death's door. Shortly afterwards, there came to see him a man, who gave himself out to be a doctor, and, having felt his pulse, he said that the poor fellow would die of his illness. The others who were by the bed were saying to one another: "He is about to breathe his last; his feet are getting cold; he has the death rattle; his eyes are becoming glassy." And then, all together: "He is dead. Let us close his eyes, let us lay his body in the coffin, and let us take him to be buried." And then: "What a misfortune, what a loss for us! He was a good man, and he was our friend." They were pretending to console one another, and the fool, who was remaining still as if he were really dead, became convinced that he was dead.

The young men placed him on a bier, and started crossing the city, and whenever the passersby asked what was going on, they replied that they were taking Nigniaca's body to be buried. Along the way many people participated in the jest, saying that they were taking Nigniaca to the cemetery. At a certain point a tavern keeper broke in with these words: "He certainly was a rogue; he was a notorious thief, and he should have been hanged!"

Whereupon the simpleton, who had heard those words, raised his head and replied: "If instead of being dead, I were alive, I would tell you, you scoundrel, that you are lying through your teeth!"

The pallbearers burst out laughing and left him in the coffin.

## 59
### *A quick repartee*

༜ TWO friends were walking through the streets of Florence and were conversing. One of them was lanky and stout; he was ugly and of dark complexion. At one point he saw a young woman who was walking along with her mother, and he said in jest: "That young girl is beautiful and graceful."

Irked by these words, the young woman replied: "One couldn't say the same about you."

"Of course one could," retorted the former, "if he only wanted to lie, as I did with you."

## 60
### *Reply of a poor man*
### *to a rich man who was cold*

༜ DURING the winter a rich man, all bundled up in his clothes, was going to Bologna. Over a mountain pass he came across a peasant who was wearing only a tattered shirt. Stunned by the fact that that man could stand the frigid weather (it was snowing and the wind was blowing), he asked him whether he wasn't frozen stiff. "Not at all," replied the other cheerfully. And when the rich man added that he was amazed by his reply because he was cold in spite of the furs he was wearing, the peasant replied: "If you wore all the clothes you own, the way I do mine, you wouldn't feel cold."

## 61

### A protest to Facino Cane for a theft

A CERTAIN man went to Facino Cane,[24] who was a cruel man and one of the most remarkable captains of our time, to protest because one of his soldiers had held him up on the road and stolen his coat. Noticing that the man was wearing a most handsome doublet, Facino asked him whether he had worn it on the day he had been robbed. The other said that he had. Whereupon Facino said: "Get out of here! The man who robbed you couldn't possibly have been one of my soldiers, for no soldier of mine would ever have left you that doublet."

## 62

### Of a man who wanted his wife to think he was dead

IN Montevarchi,[25] a village near here, a truck farmer of my acquaintance had a young wife. One day he returned home while his wife had gone to wash clothes; and as he was curious to know what she would say and do if he were to die, he threw himself on the floor and pretended to be dead. When the wife returned home loaded with the washing and found her husband dead, or so it seemed to her, for she thought he was dead, she was undecided on whether she should weep over the death of her husband or first eat a bite, since it was noon and she had not eaten anything the whole morning. Hunger won out: she placed a slice of salted meat on the fire and then began eating it hastily without stopping to drink anything. As the salted meat made her very thirsty, she took a bottle and went quickly down into the cellar to get some wine. In the meantime, a woman neighbor of hers came in to ask for some embers; the wife dropped the bottle and came up into the house; and, as if her husband had just passed on, she began weeping bitterly and lamenting over his sudden death. Attracted by her shouts and laments, all the neighbors arrived and were stunned by the man's sudden death.

The husband, stretched out on the floor, held his breath and kept his eyes closed as if he were really dead. When he thought that the joke had gone far enough, as his wife kept on weeping and repeating: "Oh, my husband, what am I going to do now?", he said opening his eyes: "You are going to be in bad shape if you do not hurry up and get some wine!"

## 63
### *Wise reply to a slanderer*

ℰ LUIGI MARSILI,[26] an Augustinian monk and a man of outstanding wisdom and learning, recently lived in Florence. In his old age he had instructed in the humanities a young man named John, who came from my hometown and whom I knew. Through the teaching of Luigi Marsili, eventually John too became a very learned man.

A Florentine fellow student of his (the old scholar had many disciples) was envious and began speaking badly of John to their teacher, saying that John was

very ungrateful and that he thought and spoke badly
of him. He did that many times, and the old teacher,
who was a man of great prudence, asked him: "How
long have you known John?" The slanderer replied
that he had known him hardly one year. Whereupon
the teacher continued: "I am surprised that you esteem
yourself so wise and me so stupid as to believe that in
one year you have learned about John's nature and
ways better than I have in ten!"

## 64

### Dispute between two young men
### who had the same coat of arms

A GENOESE, who was master of a large galley that
was fighting on behalf of the King of France against
the English, carried a shield with an ox's head painted
on it. A French nobleman saw it and said that that was
his own coat of arms. Bitter words ensued, and the
Frenchman challenged the Genoese to a duel. The latter
accepted the challenge and came on the field without
any accouterment; the former arrived with the greatest
pomp.

The Genoese then said: "For what reason have we
come here to fight?"

The other one said: "I claim that your coat of arms
is mine, and that it belonged to my ancestors before it
belonged to yours." And when the Genoese asked him
what was the emblem on his shield, he replied: "An ox's
head."

"In that case," the Genoese went on, "there is no
reason for us to duel, because the one on mine is not
an ox's head, but a cow's head." With this witty reply
he deflated the vain ostentation of the Frenchman.

## 65
### *Of a fool who derided a Florentine gentleman*

ONCE there was in Florence a gentleman of my acquaintance who was very short and wore a very long beard. A crazy fellow began making fun of his size and his beard every time he ran into him on the street. He was so troublesome that he annoyed the poor man no end.

When the gentleman's wife learned about this, she had the crazy fellow go to her house; she stuffed him with good food, gave him a suit of clothes, and begged him never to make fun of her husband again. He promised he wouldn't; and when he met him on a few occasions, he went on his way without a single remark. Those who happened to be present were completely amazed and goaded him to say something; and they asked why he did not say the same things he used to. And he said to them: "He has sealed my mouth in such a way that I will never be able to speak of him again."

## 66
### *Of a Florentine who always lied*

IN FLORENCE there was a man who was so accustomed to telling lies that his mouth never uttered the truth. A fellow who often was in his company and had become used to his lies once ran into him and, before he even opened his mouth, said to him: "You are lying!"

"What do you mean, I'm lying?" said the man, "I haven't said a thing!"

"I meant," the other fellow went on, "if you had spoken."

## 67
### Reply of a confessor to
### Bernabò Visconti concerning a woman

❧ BERNABÒ [1323–1385], Duke of Milan, was a man
much given to women. One day when he was in his
garden enjoying himself with a woman he loved, he
suddenly saw before him a friar, who was his confessor
and who, because of his great authority and knowledge,
had all the doors of the palace open to him.

The Duke blushed and became angry at the unexpected visit of his confessor; and in order to catch him
at his word, he said to him with a certain resentment:
"What would you do if you found in your bed a woman
as lovely as this one?" And the friar replied: "I know
what I ought not do, but I cannot say what I would do."

With this answer he calmed the Duke's anger, confessing that he was a man and that like other men he
might yield to temptation.

## 68
### Of a monk who in war time
### spoke of peace to Bernabò

❧ DURING the last war that the Florentines fought
against the Duke of Milan, the death penalty was decreed against anyone who should talk of peace.

Bernardo Manetti, who was a most witty man, was
at the Old Market one day buying I do not know what
when he was approached by one of those monks who go
through the streets of town and post themselves at
crossroads, soliciting alms for their needs. Before asking him for alms, the monk said to Bernardo: "Pax tibi"

["Peace be with you"] ; whereupon Bernardo said to him: "How dare you speak of peace! Don't you know that anyone who speaks of peace puts his head at stake? I am getting out of here; I don't want them to think that I am an accomplice of yours!" And so he left him and avoided being pestered by that bothersome fellow.

# II

## *Ludovico Carbone*

*1435-1482*

# CARBONE

LUDOVICO CARBONE was born in Ferrara, one of the most brilliant centers of the Italian Renaissance. He was the pupil of the illustrious humanist Guarino da Verona. When he was only twenty years of age, Carbone was appointed professor of eloquence and poetry at the university of his native city. Although it seems that he taught also in Bologna, he spent most of his life in Ferrara under the protection of Borso and Ercole d'Este.

Carbone wrote several works, both in Latin and Italian. The most important are a translation into Italian of Sallust's histories and a collection of 138 pleasantries, of which only 108 are extant.

Carbone's pleasantries are especially important because they constitute the first collection written in Italian: it seems that they were written between 1466–1471, and they were dedicated to Duke Borso d'Este of Ferrara. About seventy of Carbone's anecdotes deal with people and events of the author's time; the others, which are less interesting for us, were derived from classical sources and deal with such "standard" figures as Plato, Diogenes, Brutus, Aristippus, and so on.

Carbone derived many of his modern stories from Poggio; others he paraphrased from old motifs, or he gathered from oral tradition. This group of his facetiae speak of Dante, Cosimo de' Medici, Niccolò d'Este, Francesco Sforza, Pope Nicholas V, his master Guarino da Verona, and so on.

Although Carbone's facetiae are of little artistic significance and lack the wit and sparkle of Poggio's, they are important historically.

## *How to catch a roasted quail*

FATHER AGOSTINO, a Franciscan friar, was at the table of Monsignor Pietro da Noceto, who was the chief secretary of Pope Nicholas. When he saw that only the important guests were served quails, pheasants, partridges, and other delicious dishes, and that he was left high and dry, he decided to attain his goal with a jest. He asked one of the waiters how those quails had been caught, and the waiter replied: "We catch them in various ways, but these were caught with a certain bone instrument tied with a piece of hide, which is called a quail pipe." "I understand," said the friar; and the following day he came to the dinnertable with one of these quail pipes. And when the guests began eating, he started playing softly, first giving out one quack, then two, then three.

Monsignor Pietro, who was seated gravely like a second pope, said with an angry voice: "That certainly sounds like a quail pipe; what kind of a disturbance is that? I want to know who that brazen fool is."

Without hesitation, Father Agostino said: "I am the one: I was trying to see if I could catch one of those quails of yours."

Monsignor caught on, and a whole covey of quails flew to the friar's plate, making the use of the quail pipe no longer necessary. Whereupon the good friar said: "I want you to know, Monsignor Pietro, that all mouths are sisters, and that friars enjoy good morsels better than other people do, for they are trained in the knowledge of the supreme good."

## 2
### *Last year's sausages were better*

 MASTER ORAZIO, who was an excellent doctor, one day asked his wife: "Why is it, dear wife, that last year you made a few sausages, and they were all good; and this year you made a lot, and they are all bad?"

The wise woman replied: "Tell me, Master Orazio, do all your patients recover? You must remember that I also have other things to think about, such as going to hear a sermon, or to confession; and I cannot devote my whole attention and care to sausages, just as you, who should devote all your attention to curing the sick, instead spend your time talking of the wars of the Venetians, of the Duke of Milan, of the Florentines, of Duke John, of the Turks, and so on."

"You are right, my dear," said Master Orazio and dropped the subject altogether.

## 3
### *They had more faith than the Pope*

 POPE JOHN XXIII,[1] who found no joy in spiritual matters and who was devoted more to the things of this world than to the fear of God or to religion, seeing a group of barefooted monks who lived very poorly for the love of God and the hope of eternal glory, turned to them, saying: "You poor simpletons! How you would be cheated if our faith turned out to be false!"

## 4
### *A quick repartee of Dante*

꙾ DANTE ALIGHIERI, the Florentine poet, was very quick with repartees. Since he had a speculative and contemplative mind, one day while hearing Mass, whether he did it because he was completely absorbed by some subtle fantasy or in order to mock his friends, at the elevation of the Body of Christ he did not kneel down, nor did he remove his hood. His rivals, for he had many because he was a worthy man, ran at once to the Bishop to accuse Dante of heresy and of having failed to pay reverence to the Sacrament. The Bishop called Dante and rebuked him. He asked the poet what he had done when the host was being elevated.

Dante replied: "To tell you the truth, I was collected so in the thought of God that I do not recall what my body did; however, those bad men, whose eyes and mind were concentrating more on me than on God, will be able to tell you; if they had turned their minds to God, they would not have spent their time watching what I was doing."

## 5
### *The most powerful of medicines*

꙾ SEEING that the medicines he was taking made him feel worse and worse as days went by, a sick man decided to stop taking them and to let nature take its course. He had all the potions the doctor sent him placed under his bed, and then he made the doctor believe that he had drunk them. Thus, with the grace of God, every day he kept getting better; the doctor felt that he was responsible for it and praised his medicines. When the patient was almost completely well, the doctor said to him: "In order that you may get back on your feet as soon as possible, I will give you one last medicine, which will make you completely well." But the patient hid it with the rest of them. The doctor returned to visit him; and, seeing that he was entirely recovered, thanked God and his own medicines.

Whereupon, the good man said: "Undoubtedly, messere, your medicines are really powerful, for they healed me from under my bed; I am convinced that if I had drunk them all, they would have made me immortal." He took out the washbasin in which he had collected all the potions and returned them to the doctor, asking him to take them away because he no longer needed them.

## 6

### *He was happy he had gone blind*

BECAUSE of his excessive addiction to lust, Febo dal Sarasino was gradually losing his eyesight. When he turned completely blind, he said: "The Lord be praised; now I will be able to indulge all I want without fear of going blind."

## 7

### *"Accipitrem" does not mean "Archpriest!"*

OUR Duke [2] had a letter written to Polo da Foiano, who was mayor of Carpaneto, in the Modena district. This letter, which was written in Latin, said that he should catch a sparrow hawk and send it to him tied up inside a sack, so that it would not get away. The letter read as follows: "Dilectissime noster, capias accipitrem et mitte nobis ligatum in sacculo ne aufugiat." [*"Dear friend, catch a sparrow hawk and send it to us tied in a small sack, so that it will not get away."*] The Mayor, who knew rustic grammar, upon reading the word *accipitrem* ["hawk"], took it to mean *arciprete* ["archpriest"] and called his son-in-law Pavaione and said: "Our lord wrote me, and he wants me to catch the archpriest and to send him to him tied up in a sack, so that he will not flee; he must be guilty of some treachery! Read this letter."

Pavaione, who knew just about as much grammar as his uncle, read the letter and said: "There is no doubt that *accipitrem* means the archpriest; but don't mention a word of this to the notary, for he is a relative of his."

Thus they sent for the archpriest and told him that he was a prisoner of the Duke. The good man, who was innocent, replied that he was forever a prisoner of his lord, but that he was not guilty of anything.

"Well," they said, "we still must obey."

Thus, they put him into a sack and brought him to Ferrara. They went to Lodovico Casella, and they told him that they had carried out what had been requested of them.

Lodovico replied that he was ignorant of such a request and asked them: "But have you a letter?"

They replied: "Certainly," and showed him the letter.

You can imagine how much Lodovico enjoyed reading it; but not to disclose their ignorance, he said that he would check with the Duke, who sent back word that the priest be released because he had changed his mind. And I believe that from then on, letters were written only in the vulgar tongue in order to avoid a repetition of the blunder of mistaking a hawk for an archpriest!

# III

## *Piovano Arlotto*

*1396-1484*

# ARLOTTO

ARLOTTO MAINARDI, known more commonly as Piovano [Priest] Arlotto, was born in San Cresci a Maciuoli near Florence. He spent most of his life in his native town, where he was the parish priest; in his youth, however, he traveled on several occasions, as ship chaplain, to Flanders, France, London, and various Italian maritime cities.

During his lifetime, as also after his death, an anonymous friend wrote down his witticisms and pleasantries, the *Motti e facezie del Piovano Arlotto*. Priest Arlotto himself was the "father" of most of the jokes, jests, and pleasantries recorded by the anonymous author of the book, which, however, contains also several that were attributed to the witty priest by tradition.

Wise Priest Arlotto lived to a ripe old age, beloved, it seems, by all those who knew him: from his simple parishioners to the members of the Medici family and their circle of scholars and artists. In some ways, Arlotto had certain characteristics of wit and humor that are reminiscent of the buffoons who, during the Renaissance, brought gaity to the various Italian courts, like the Gonnella made famous by Franco Sacchetti, the writer of novelle; but he was quite different from them in his deep-seated practical wisdom and knowledge of the frailties of human nature. Arlotto's book of pleasantries indicates that our priest was a sensible, human individual who loved the pleasures of the table but was an enemy of excesses of all kinds. He accepted philosophically the ups and downs of daily existence and judged everybody and everything without prejudices and with an open mind. He saw the serious, but also the comical side of life.

Priest Arlotto soon became a proverbial character, and his pleasantries met with universal favor in Italy. Many of the anecdotes attributed to him are original; others are closely linked to tradition. In general, Arlotto's anecdotes are longer than the stories of Bracciolini and of other writers of facetiae; some come near to being short stories. Several of Arlotto's pleasantries are in the nature of a practical joke, such as will be later analysed by Castiglione in his *Book of the Courtier*.

Arlotto's *Motti e facezie* are written in simple, conversational, fifteenth-century Tuscan; and they are rich with details of the life and customs of the time. Later compilers of pleasantries who made use of Arlotto's collection invariably cut the long narrative down to what they considered the meaty part of a given anecdote, and their versions are therefore less interesting to us.

The first edition of the *Motti e facezie* goes back to the beginning of the sixteenth century (1514–1516?). Many were the editions that followed, either complete or partial. Arlotto's pleasantries were translated into French and German, but, oddly, never into English.

## *Priest Arlotto and the King of Naples*

ON their way to Sicily, our Florentine galleys called at Naples where they waited a few days. On one of these galleys was our Priest Arlotto; and this was at the time of that invincible, magnificent, and most liberal King Alfonso.[1] The latter knew of Arlotto, for he had heard about some of his pleasantries. King Alfonso

learned that Arlotto had brought along a book in which he recorded as debtors all those who, through lack of common sense, committed some grave blunder; and he did this without paying any attention to rank or friendship. The King immediately sent for him, gave him a warm welcome, and after he heard a few of his jests asked him whether it was true that he kept a book of blunders.

"Yes, your Sacred Majesty."

The King said: "During the last few days, have you written down as debtors any of these Neapolitans of ours?"

Priest Arlotto replied: "He who takes notes does not remember." So he sent to the galley for his book, opened it, and said: "Lord, I see a few in this book, and among them is the name of your Majesty, about whom the entry reads as follows: 'His Majesty the most glorious and invincible King Alfonso owes the following debt because of a grave blunder, namely because he sent to Germany for some horses, and he entrusted the German Teodorigo with five hundred and fifty-five gold ducats.'"

Filled with amazement, the King said: "My good Father, does this seem such a grave blunder to you? I have taken care of this fellow since he was a little boy, and he has been in this court in my service for nearly eighteen years. He has always been most faithful to me; and undoubtedly it seems to me that in this instance you haven't used good judgment, and that you have unjustly written down my name among your debtors."

The Priest replied: "Your Highness, I have treated you justly; and I don't believe there is a greater blunder in this book, especially when one considers who committed it. Could there be a greater and graver blunder than entrusting so much money to a barbarian who is penniless and who, neither here in Naples nor anywhere else, has any personal property or real estate to lose? And what is even worse, you sent him to his own homeland in Germany. Don't we see constantly that for the paltriest sum of money fathers deceive their children, children deceive their fathers, and brothers deceive their brothers? Haven't we seen or heard that sometimes a hermit who has spent a long time in a hermitage, leading a holy life in the midst of the harshest penance, all of a sudden, through diabolical instigation, out of avarice and wicked malice commits a murder in order to acquire money and wealth, and then leads a wicked existence until his death? Man is the most deceitful of animals, and it is impossible ever to know him."

Because of so many reasons with which Priest Arlotto justified the entry, the King no longer knew what to say and remained speechless; but after thinking a while, he asked the Priest: "Tell me, if Teodorigo returns with the horses or with the money, what will you say then?"

Without hesitating, the Priest replied: "I will erase your Majesty's name, and I will put Teodorigo down as a debtor for having committed such a greater blunder and foolishness."

2

*Priest Arlotto made a certain*
*Brother Ventura whistle while he*
*was raising the Sacrament*

BROTHER VENTURA invited Priest Arlotto to his church on the morning of the festivity of Saint Lawrence. Since he was the rector of that church, which was called the Church of St. Lawrence, he held every year a beautiful celebration. Brother Ventura was a simple, good, and upright man. On the morning of his festival, Priest Arlotto arrived at the said church of St. Lawrence and found Brother Ventura properly vested at the altar. After they had greeted each other, Brother Ventura said:

"My good Father, you couldn't have come at a better time. As you see, the altar boy wanted to serve Mass; but since you are here, you can do it. I will send him to attend to the house chores, especially in the kitchen, so that the food will be properly cooked and seasoned; for I want you and the other priests who attend the celebration this morning to have a good meal."

The Priest replied: "Last night I fasted; and you know that he who goes to bed supperless tumbles and tosses all night long."

"That being the case," Brother Ventura said, "this morning your board will be that of a mule driver."

Then he began saying Mass. After he finished reciting the Gloria, Brother Ventura turned to Priest Arlotto and asked why he had not rung the bell at the Gloria, as is customary. And the latter replied: "The clapper is broken."

Brother Ventura said: "What shall I do? Do me the favor of putting a new one in its place."

Arlotto replied: "All I have here is the one my mother gave me, and I wouldn't give you that one for your whole church."

Brother Ventura didn't see how he could go on with the Mass or raise the Sacrament without the sound of bells, and he was lamenting with Priest Arlotto over what he might do on the spur of the moment, saying: "I just can't go on and finish Mass without some sound."

Arlotto, who was anxious to test how far his simplicity went, said: "I am sorry there is nothing we can ring; since there is no other remedy, whistle with your mouth as best you can, and go on with the Mass."

When time came to raise the Sacrament, Brother Ventura whistled so loudly that he would have induced a whole herd of cattle to drink from the same trough. Thus, he made Priest Arlotto and all those who were present laugh so hard that when they think of it, they burst into laughter all over again.

## 3
### St. Cresci is not a saint for omelets

❧ WHILE his father Cosimo was still alive, Giovanni
de' Medici went one evening to Fiesole, where he had a
palace. He took along Piero de' Pazzi, Francesco Martelli, Fruosino da Panzano, and certain other noblemen.
Once they were inside the palace, they said: "What
shall we eat tonight, since it is Friday?" They asked
the cook to fix devilled eggs, plain omelets, stuffed
omelets, and eggs cooked in various other ways. But
the plain omelets and the stuffed omelets stuck to the
pan and didn't turn out right. When the cook brought
them to the table, Giovanni said to him:

"You seem to have forgotten how to cook; don't you
see how peculiar these omelets look?"

"What can I do about it if the pan isn't working
right?"

"Go and prepare four more," Giovanni replied, "and
make a vow to the saint of Priest Arlotto, namely St.
Cresci: and if he grants you that they turn out well,
tomorrow you can go to his shrine and place before him
a candle worth a *grosso*,[2] which I will give you."

In order to win his reputation back and also because
the grosso was not coming out of his pocket, the cook
made his vow devotedly and prepared more omelets.
They turned out worse than before. Giovanni and the
others had to be satisfied with them the way they were.
Once they were back in Florence, the following Mon-
day they ran into Priest Arlotto; they told him the
whole story and they complained bitterly that his Saint
Cresci had refused to bestow a favor upon them.

The Priest replied to them angrily and said: "Aren't

you ashamed of having such a low opinion of my saint?
He treated you the way you deserved. Do you think
he is a saint for plain and stuffed omelets? Break a
shoulder, or a thigh, or your head, and you will see
what he can do for you then!"

## 4

### *Priest Arlotto confesses a peasant*

❦ ON A holy Wednesday a young peasant came to the
church of Priest Arlotto and said: "Father, I should
like to confess my sins."

The Priest made him kneel and asked him about his
sins; and he found that he had committed quite a lot
of them. Among his many sins, the peasant confessed
that he had committed over two hundred thefts and
that he had stolen from the poor as well as from the
rich. At one point he said, "About six months ago, on
a rainy night I came to your house three times and stole
three bushels and three-quarters-and-one-half of wheat."

The Priest said: "That was worse [than all your
other sins]. That night I missed it all right, and I was
very upset."

The peasant went on confessing a large number of
other sins; and after about half an hour, he stopped and
remained silent as if struck.

He had been in a trance for a while when Priest
Arlotto said: "What are you doing? Why aren't you
talking? What are you thinking about? Do you want
to say anything else?"

He sighed deeply several times but did not say anything.

The Priest asked him again: "Do you have anything
else to confess?"

He said, weeping and sobbing at the same time: "My Father, the devil holds me back; and it's out of shame that I do not dare mention a horrible, wicked, and unpardonable sin; I have never confessed it, and I don't believe that God will ever be willing to forgive me for it."

"My son, I don't want you to do that again; but what sin can it possibly be that you refuse to confess? Don't you know that our Lord Jesus Christ endured many torments and sorrows; and then, at the end, he chose to die so ignominiously on the cross for us wretched sinners? His mercy is so great that he is ever holding His arms open to receive sinners, as long as they are willing to confess their sins and repent and do humble penance for them. However grave a sin may be, He always forgives it: even if you have robbed hospitals and altars and have murdered one thousand men and done the greatest evil, provided you confess all this, do your penance with devotion and contrition, and make whatever amends you can, our most clement God remits your sins. Now, for the love of God do not hesitate to confess this sin and any other you may recall; speak freely and have no doubts." And Priest Arlotto thought that it must be some unheard of, nefarious, and unpardonable sin.

After that long sermon, the youth said: "My Father, although I am not willing, I shall tell you. When I was a boy of fifteen, through idleness and the evil temptation of the flesh, a few times I took my beater promenading and I fed him oats in such a way that I derived great pleasure from it."

The Priest burst out laughing and said: "Take your beater out promenading as often as you like, but do not steal any more; leave other people's property alone, and above all give me my wheat back!"

## 5

### *The man who spat near the altar*

❦ THERE was a troublesome man of about fifty-five
years of age who, out of devotion, every morning at
nine o'clock went to hear Mass at the holy church of
the Annunziata.[3] He knelt by the side of the altar; and,
with little reverence, he took off a rose-colored cap that
he folded to keep it from getting soiled, and every
day, without fail, he put it on the altar. Then, since
he suffered from catarrh, he chewed, mumbled, and
spat right at the foot of the altar; and every morning
he made such a puddle that it would have almost filled
a jug. The monks of the church were so vexed at him
that when he was in the church, it had become almost
impossible to find anyone who was willing to go and
say or serve Mass; nor did they dare say anything to
him because he was a well-known public figure.

While the monks were in this quandary, the prior
was thinking of finding a solution. One day he met
Priest Arlotto; they exchanged greetings, and then the
prior said: "This morning I'd like you to come and,
out of devotion, say your Mass at the altar of the
blessed Annunziata; then you will come and partake
of the customary lunch with us monks."

The Priest accepted; he went into the sacristy; and,
since it was by then exactly nine o'clock, he put on the
vestments. Our man was already in church.

As the Priest was beginning to say Mass, the man,
in his usual fashion, put his cap on the altar and began
to spit. The Priest saw this incredible beast and marveled at his insolence; furthermore, the noise he made
with his spitting was so loud that it was difficult to
proceed with Mass. When he came to the Preface, at

the point when the Priest opens out his arms, he made a certain gesture with his hand so that he knocked the man's cap to the ground; and it so happened that it landed on the lake he had made with his spit.

The man rose to his feet infuriated and went to the sacristy where he cleaned his cap as well as he could. When Priest Arlotto finished Mass, he came into the sacristy to remove his vestments, and the worthy citizen said to him:

"Father, you soiled this cap of mine; but I forgive you because you did it not realizing what you were doing."

The Priest said: "Are you so dense that you believe that I did not notice your madness and your insolence? I saw perfectly well what I did. Aren't you ashamed of putting your cap and your lice on the altar near the chalice, and of vomiting the whole morning long so recklessly that more than once I was afraid you would fill the chalice with something else besides water and wine? I can tell you that if I were to come here every day like these monks, it wouldn't take me long to cure you of this habit of yours."

The man was filled with shame and went away without saying another word. Those who were in the sacristy laughed their sides off. The monks gave Priest Arlotto his lunch and thanked him for the lesson he had taught the worthy citizen.

## 6

### The Mass for hunters

EARLY one morning some young men came to Priest Arlotto and said, "Father, we are in a hurry because we have to go to a place that is very important to us; and we should like you to say a quick Mass for us.

You know what we mean, of course: say for us a Mass for hunters."

The Priest vested himself slowly, and then he began. After he had said the Introit and the Confession, he stopped and began turning the pages of the missal. The young men couldn't understand why he was not going on with the Mass, nor why he wasn't saying anything else. After a long while, they did not know what to do; and, being on pins and needles and in a great hurry, they said:

"Father, what are you doing? You keep on turning the pages, and you are not going on with the Mass."

"This morning you are driving me out of my mind," the Priest said. "I have been looking all through this missal, and I just cannot find a Mass for hunters. If you want me to say one of the Masses that is in this missal, I will say it; otherwise, I will stop right here, and I will take my vestments off."

The young men realized their error and allowed him to say the Mass that was customary for that day.

## 7

### *A story that Piero, son of Cosimo de' Medici, told Priest Arlotto*

SOMETIMES, as an act of charity, Priest Arlotto went to visit Piero, son of Cosimo de' Medici, who was bedridden with the gout. They liked to see each other because they liked each other; and they always exchanged pleasantries.

One day Piero told him this story: in Florence there was at one time a shoemaker who did not have much money and who very devotedly went every day, early in the morning, to recite certain prayers in the church of St. Michael Berteldi. He went before an altar, which was in said church, upon which was the statue of St. John the Baptist.

This had been going on for a long time, every morning at dawn, when an unkind and mischievous altar server decided to hear what the shoemaker said to Saint John so early in the morning.

One morning he slipped behind the altar and placed himself behind the statue. The shoemaker came, knelt before the said image, and began saying his prayers in a low voice; and the altar server could hear every one of his words. Then he said: "Dear St. John, I pray you that you grant me two things: first, I should like to know whether my wife has ever betrayed me; secondly, I should like to know what my son will become when he grows up."

The altar server heard everything and replied in a gentle voice: "I want you to know, my son, that because of your long devotion to me, your wish will be granted. Come back here tomorrow morning and you will have the correct answers. Go in peace."

The foolish shoemaker left; and believing that what he had heard was the voice of St. John, he was very happy.

Early the following morning the shoemaker returned to get his answer; and after he had recited his prayers, he said: "St. John, keep your promise."

The altar server had hidden himself again behind the statue of St. John, and in his turn he began speaking softly and said as follows: "My faithful servant, I reply to you that your son will soon be hanged and that your wife has betrayed you with more than one man."

The shoemaker rose to his feet and began walking away in high dudgeon without saying anything else.

But when he had gone half way down the aisle, he turned around and went back to the altar; and, without kneeling or doffing his hat, he said:

"What kind of a St. John are you?"

"I am your John the Baptist," replied the altar server, who was still there.

In his firm belief that the voice had come from the statue, the shoemaker said full of anger and indignation: "The Devil take you! You always spoke nothing but evil, and because of your wicked tongue Herod had your head cut off. I know that you haven't told me the truth about anything I have asked; I have been coming here to worship you for over twenty-five years, and I have never been a burden to you. You may be sure that I shall never come back to see you again."

8

*A story that Priest Arlotto*
*told Piero, son of Cosimo de' Medici*

AFTER Piero, son of Cosimo, told the above story to Priest Arlotto, he said: "You are my debtor; pay up."

And the Priest replied: "I have no other debts, so I want to pay this one before I leave your house." So before going he began telling a charming story as follows:

Not many years ago in this city of ours, namely Florence, there was a good, poor doublet maker who had a shop near the oratory of Or' San Michele; and every day toward midmorning, out of devotion, he went to said oratory and lighted a candle before a holy painting. On this painting was the image of Christ, when as a boy he was disputing with the priests in the temple and his mother was looking for him. Every morning the doublet maker recited a few prayers devotedly.

He had been doing this for well over twenty-five years when one day his son, who was watching a ball game, was hit on the head by a roof tile and was seriously wounded. He sent for doctors and medicines, for his boy was in critical condition.

The following morning the doublet maker went as usual to Or' San Michele and, instead of a small penny candle, he lit before the image of Christ a large candle worth one grosso. He recited his usual prayers, and then he said these words:

"My sweet Lord Jesus Christ, I entreat you to heal my boy. You know that in twenty-five years of devotion to you I have never asked anything of you. All I have is this boy, who is my only offspring, and he too has been devoted to you. If he should die, I would die of despair. I implore you."

Then he left the church: he returned home, and shortly after, his boy departed from this world.

The following day the doublet maker went to Or' San Michele early in the morning. He was filled with anger because of the death of his son; he went straight to the image of Christ, but he did not bring a candle; he did not kneel, nor did he say the customary prayers. On the contrary, he began complaining as follows:

"I take back all my devotion, and I never want to come before you again. You know that I have been faithful to you for over twenty-five years; I never asked but one favor of you, and you refused to grant it. If I had asked this favor of that large crucifix that is next to you, my prayer would have been granted. I promise that I shall never again have anything to do with you or with other children, for he who gets mixed up with children can only expect childish behavior!"

## 9
### Witticism of Arlotto in the church of Santo Spirito

❦ ONE morning Priest Arlotto was walking through the church of Santo Spirito in Florence, and he saw a woman who was heaving deep sighs and saying her prayers devotedly before an image of Saint Nicholas of Tolentino. She had been praying and gesticulating in that manner for perhaps one whole hour, and she seemed spellbound.

Priest Arlotto went to her, seized her by the head, and turned her in the direction of an image of the crucified Christ that was nearby; and he said:

"Can't you see, you foolish woman, that you are making a big mistake? Address your prayers to Him who is the Master and can help you better than His pupil."

## 10
### Jest on the death of Leonardo Aretino

❦ PRIEST ARLOTTO was passing by the Uccellatoio.[4] He stopped to talk with the innkeeper Agnolo about certain matters; then he got off his horse and went into the stable, where he was overtaken by a man who, out of breath and filled with anxiety, greeted the priest and said: "For the love of God, buy me a pint of wine; for I am very thirsty!"

The Priest, filled with amazement, said: "Aren't you messer Leonardo from Arezzo?"[5]

"Yes, I am."

The Priest inquired: "What are you doing here so

early, and how does it happen you are so alone and so anguished?"

He replied: "Can't you see that I am dead? I am on my way, and I cannot remain here with you; I am in such a calamity that I am racked by thirst, and I do not have the money to pay for a little wine. Won't you help me?"

The Priest asked: "How can that be possible? How can you have died so poor? According to the opinion of many people, you owned so much land and so many houses that they were valued at twenty thousand ducats; your books, furniture, jewels, and clothes were valued at over twenty-five thousand, and your cash at over thirty thousand ducats. Where is the knowledge, the wisdom, the learning, the eloquence of Greek and Latin letters? Where is the Ciceronian style that lighted up the whole world? Is it possible that Fame and all those Muses who were all obedient to you have abandoned you, and that now you leave in such a state?"

The soul of messer Leonardo replied: "Dear Father, I have left behind much more property and a richer treasure than you have just mentioned; but you must believe me when I tell you that I have been completely abandoned by everybody, and that I cannot take into the next world a single farthing. I am leaving behind my body and all my possessions. And since you are remaining in this world, I advise you to keep in God's grace and to have a good time as long as you live; for when you die you will not be able to take anything with you. See what happened to me. Woe is me! Think of how troubled I must be. I am going, and I do not know what my fate will be; for I haven't as yet appeared before the Judge. I am trembling; I am freezing; I am burning; and I do not know yet who will judge me and what judgment will be passed on me. I am seriously concerned, since I am well aware of the life I have led, and especially of my sin of avarice. In order to accumulate money and possessions, I did not hesitate to draw up the most wicked of contracts. I worked very hard, and I never satisfied the slightest of my whims. Now I leave all my wealth to my children, and Heaven knows how long they will hold on to it! Goodby, dear Father; remain in peace. Enjoy yourself; have a good time, and do not do as I did." And he left.

Stunned and frightened out of his wits, Priest Arlotto remained frozen to the spot for a quarter of an hour. When he regained his senses, he mounted his horse and returned to Florence. Once at home, he quickly changed his clothes and went to see Domenico from Figline and Luta, two boon companions of his, and told them the whole incident. He wept as he related to them the sad story of messer Leonardo, and he concluded:

"Let us learn from his example; let us do our best to enjoy ourselves and to do and keep doing good. As you see, when death comes to us, we cannot take anything with us. In so far as I am concerned, I want to follow the advice of that holy man, Brother Jacopone da Todi, who in one of his hymns, which is full of precepts and maxims, has the following saying: 'That much is mine that I enjoy and give in the name of God.' "

## II

### *The parable of malmsey wine*

PRIEST ARLOTTO and Bartolomeo Sassetti went to have lunch at the house of that upright man by the name of Francesco Dini.[6]

After they sat down at the table, Francesco said: "Father, I have some malmsey wine; would you like it before lunch or after?"

He replied in parable form, saying: "The blessed Virgin Mary was a virgin before delivery, during delivery, and after delivery."

Being an intelligent and generous man, Francesco saw to it that nothing but malmsey wine was served during the meal.

## 12

### *Jest made by Priest Arlotto at Pontassieve on a cold evening*

❧ ONE SUNDAY evening, on his way back from the Casentino,[7] Priest Arlotto stopped for the night at an inn in Pontassieve.[8] He was drenched, tired, cold, and covered with mud, for it had rained the whole day.

After he dismounted his horse, he went before a roaring fire that the innkeeper had lighted for him; and there he found about thirty peasants; for, in addition to the rain, it was cold. On holidays, it is customary with peasants to spend the whole day and evening at the inn—drinking, gambling, and telling their coarse stories and lies.

That evening they were crowded around that fire, and they were practically on top of Priest Arlotto in such a way that the poor man could neither dry himself nor get warm, and only with great difficulty was he able to turn around. It was useless for him and the innkeeper to talk to those peasants; they refused to budge.

The Priest, who was filled with indignation, worked out a plan to drive those peasants from the fire. He assumed a dejected and afflicted countenance: he did not laugh at anything; he did not speak; he did not quip. The innkeeper was completely stunned by this, for he knew that the Priest was always gay and cheerful, whereas that evening he hardly said a word; and so he said:

"Father, what's the matter with you this evening?
You look dazed, and this is contrary to your cheerful
and merry nature. If you are ill, or if something troubles
you, tell me; for there is nothing I and my relatives
wouldn't do for you." The innkeeper was wondering
whether he might have been abused by someone in the
Casentino, for those peasants are bad people.

The Priest replied: "I had the misfortune of losing
about fourteen silver lire and nineteen gold florins from
this bag, but I have hope of finding a few of them; for
I know that they must have dropped out of my bag no
more than five miles away from here. I stopped for a
drink of wine about five miles back; and after I had
gone half a mile I stopped to pass some water and as
I got back on my horse, my bag was ripped by a tack
in the saddle. Those coins dropped out of my bag
through that tear one by one, and I know that due to
the bad weather no one else has come along that road.
I want you to do me a favor: tomorrow morning early,
if it does not rain, I want you to go with me or send
someone with me to look for my money."

The Priest had hardly finished saying these words
when those peasants began filing out in groups of two,
four, and six, until not one of them was left. They
whispered to one another some mysterious words, and
they decided then and there to go and look for that
money and steal it from the Priest. Heedless of the
bad weather and without wasting any time, for it was
still raining hard, they went in search of the money
with torches and lanterns, and hoods on their heads;
and along with them went one of the innkeeper's sons
and three of his nephews. They all spent a miserable
night, however, and several of them came down with
a wretched fever. Our Priest was left to enjoy the fire
with room to spare, and those peasants found that
money in their dreams.

## 13

### *The cleanest craftsmen in the world*

ONE evening during supper they were talking about various things, and at one point someone suggested that everyone give his opinion on which are the cleanest craftsmen. Many were the opinions expressed: some praised one craft, others another.

Priest Arlotto said: "I hold a completely different opinion from all of you, and I say that kilnmen are the cleanest of all craftsmen."

They all began laughing and winking at one another over the foolish and senseless judgment they thought the Priest had passed.

The Priest said: "I know that you are laughing at me. Nonetheless I do not wish to change my mind; and I state that kilnmen, who are always handling clay, bricks, and lime, are the cleanest craftsmen in the world, because before they go to the toilet, they never fail to wash their hands."

## 14

### *Questions that Priest Arlotto put to a man he had judged wise*

ONE day Priest Arlotto was conversing with a group of people, among whom was a man whom he judged to be a wise person and who began asking senseless and unreasonable questions, such as: "Why didn't God do thus and so? He should have done in such and such a manner. Why didn't He make us all Christians? Why did He make Jews and Mohammedans?"

After he had chattered for a while, Arlotto said:

"I have no intention of putting theological questions or problems before you, but I should like you to explain some simple matters. Why is it that the grape is given such little protection that every tiny dewdrop damages and spoils it; and yet it is such a noble fruit that it produces a sublime beverage, and it gives valuable nourishment; whereas the pine seed, which is not so noble or so valuable, is protected by an armor of hard spiny scales? And I'd like to ask you something else: why is it that the calf of the leg is not located in front of the shin, which is often hit and has no protection whatsoever, whereas the calf is never injured? Further, I should like to learn from you for what reason the dung of the ox is not as sweet and noble as that of the bee; for it seems to me that it should be the opposite, and also that in many instances, especially in the three I have mentioned, nature was blind. I should like to hear your opinion."

As the man did not know what to say, the Priest concluded: "This should prove to you that you are out of your mind in insisting to discuss and defend theological questions when you are unable to explain such simple matters."

## 15

### The sermon on Don Lupo

ONCE our galleys were carrying certain Catalan gentlemen from Naples to Catalonia. One of them, whose name was Don Lupo ["Mr. Wolf"], took sick, and after a few days he died. They dropped anchor in a town, and they honored the departed in the manner of that land; but the captain asked Priest Arlotto to deliver a sermon in honor of the dead man, as was customary in Florence.

The Priest climbed into the pulpit and spoke as follows: "I have been chosen undeservedly to preach here: however, to comply with the command of our captain and to please the other noblemen here present, I shall say a few words. Fear God and observe his

commandments. It is customary to say a few things in praise of the departed, when he has left a good name behind in this world. Among other animals there are four that have this merit and characteristic: one is good alive but not dead, and this is the donkey; the other is good dead but not alive, and this is the hog; the other is good both alive and dead, and this is the ox; the other, which is the fourth one, is neither good alive nor dead, and this is the wolf.

"This body before us was named Lupo, and he was a Catalan to boot; I really do not know what good I can say of him, and therefore I shall say nothing and will bring my sermon to a close. *Pax et benedictio, amen."*

## 16

### *Priest Arlotto confesses a sick tailor*

A TAILOR, who was a friend of Priest Arlotto, had lived next door to him in Florence for a long time. He was considered a good craftsman in his profession, but he was known as a wicked man and a thief.

The Priest had reprimanded him a few times, but to little avail. It so happened that one day he came down with a dangerous, lingering fever that lasted about three months. He was growing worse from day to day, but he did not want to confess his sins, nor to take communion; and the Priest rebuked him repeatedly.

As he was persisting in his obstinacy, he dreamed one night of a man with a flag in his hand, who invited him to follow him. The flag seemed painted with all sorts of colors, practically with all the colors imaginable.

When he woke the next morning, he was filled with fear and he sent for Priest Arlotto and told him the whole thing.

The Priest replied: "You are obstinate; every day you grow worse, and still you refuse to make your peace with God. If you confess yourself, I shall tell you the meaning of your vision."

Either through fear or because of the entreaties and threats of the Priest, he consented to confess himself; and after his confession, the Priest told him that the man he had seen was the devil, and that the colors represented all the various kinds of cloth he had stolen in cutting dresses and gowns. Whereupon the tailor confessed that he had been stealing for nearly fifty years.

"You will have to return what you have stolen," the Priest said.

The tailor replied: "That's not possible, I wouldn't be able to return one penny's worth. Indeed, the whole neighborhood wouldn't be able to return what I have stolen during the last fifty years; for I can assure you that I never cut a single piece of cloth, small though it was, that I didn't steal at least a span for a pair of cuffs. If I could, I'd be glad to return everything."

"All right, then; but see, at least, that you stop stealing."

"I couldn't do that either, because I am so accustomed to taking a bit of cloth for myself, that while cutting I wouldn't stop and think. Yet, if I could think about it, I wouldn't steal a single thing."

The Priest said: "I'll tell you what to do so that you will always remember. I am convinced that, like a faithful Christian, you have made a true confession; but since you are so steeped in evil and in stealing, see to it that when you are cutting you have with you a workman. In order to protect your honor, I don't want you to tell him anything about this matter; simply warn him that, when he sees you seize the scissors to cut the cloth, he must tell you: 'Master, that flag!' In this manner I know that you will remember to do your duty, and you will not sin."

The tailor said: "That's good advice; I thank you, and I promise you to follow it."

Presently the tailor recovered his health and began going back to his shop; and every time he was cutting, he had by his side sometimes an errand boy, other times an apprentice, who as soon as the tailor brought the scissors down on the material would say: "Master, that flag!" Whereupon, the tailor, who had reached out for more material than was required, brought the scissors back to the correct marking, and did his duty.

Not much time later, there came to Florence a gentleman from another town; and he bought many fine fabrics and an expensive cut of gold brocade. It so happened that Priest Arlotto had become acquainted with this gentleman, who showed great friendship toward him. To show his good will toward the tailor, Priest Arlotto saw to it that the latter was asked to make a gown out of the gold brocade for that gentleman. As soon as the tailor took the scissors in his hand to cut the brocade, he realized that it was a magnificent piece of cloth; he reached out with his hand as far as he could, and immediately his apprentice cried out: "Master, that flag!" And the tailor quickly rejoined: "This color wasn't on it!"

## 17

### *A priest wished to become rich selling used balls, and Arlotto told him the story of mice*

℘ A PRIEST who was a close relative of Priest Arlotto asked him one day to let him go along on his galley. The Priest discouraged him in various ways, and told him that it wouldn't be to his advantage to go on such a voyage. But it was of no use; he said that he had some money that he wanted to invest profitably, and that he wanted to go along. And so he went with the owner of one of the galleys, which set sail with the flagship on which Priest Arlotto was traveling. When they got to Flanders, the merchants spent several months in Bruges; and during that time, the aforementioned priest constantly hovered about Arlotto.

In Bruges, as in the rest of Flanders, lawn tennis was very popular, and the tennis ball business was very active. Many people rented tennis balls. The balls were changed after each game and also after every fault. The players paid the master of the game for the balls, and the latter had a right also to all the used balls that were left on the field, so that the men who ran the lawn tennis games always had carloads of used balls for sale.

During the long time that the merchants who had come on the galleys remained in Bruges, that priest learned all about the lawn tennis ball business. He concluded that he could make a large profit himself; for, whereas in Bruges those balls were sold at three pennies for five, in Florence they could be sold at three pennies each.

Rashly and without asking for the advice of Priest Arlotto or of the others, the priest bought five large barrelfuls of balls, thus investing all his money and remaining completely penniless. Then he went to Priest Arlotto; and, grinning from ear to ear, told him about the investment he had made in tennis balls. Arlotto, who was a wise man, did not blame him for what he had done; he simply told him that once they returned to Florence, he should remind him to tell him the story of the Genoese merchant and the cats.

After the galleys docked at the port of Pisa and the Florentine merchants had returned to Florence, the priest began selling the balls; and with less than half a barrelful he stocked all the stores for several years. He was left with the rest of the balls; and if he had decided to toss them away one by one, he would have had enough to last him twenty-five years and even longer.

When the priest realized how foolish he had been and what a blunder he had made, he went to call on

Priest Arlotto and confessed that he was sorry not to have taken his advice. Then Arlotto said: "Now I will tell you the story of the Genoese merchant and the cats.

"There was a fortunate Genoese merchant who, on one of his voyages, was blown by a great storm to far away, unknown lands, where no Christian had ever been seen. He put into port on a very rich island, whose lord was a wealthy and powerful king. When the latter heard that a ship had been blown in by the storm, he was filled with amazement and repeatedly sent for the merchant inviting him for lunch. One morning the merchant accepted and went. After he arrived, and the finger bowls were passed around, everyone, including the King and Queen, was given a stick. Then they all sat down at the table with those sticks. The merchant was dumbfounded. Suddenly, as the bread and the other victuals were brought to the table, there was a great uproar: nearly one thousand mice stormed into the room and tried to snatch the food from the guests' hands; and they, by wielding their canes furiously, tried to keep the mice away.

"Completely stunned, the Genoese merchant asked the King what was the meaning of those canes, and whence those hordes of mice had come. The king said:

" 'If it weren't for this avalanche of mice, I wouldn't hesitate to say that the inhabitants of this kingdom were the happiest people in the world; for here one can find the most precious things in the world: gold, silver, all kinds of metals, oats, wheat, wine, fruit of all kinds, wax, silk, and all that the earth produces. Those cursed animals ruin everything; as you can see, we have to keep our bread and our clothes on those long hooks that dangle from the ceilings of our homes.'

"The merchant said: 'This morning your Majesty invited me to lunch; tomorrow morning I should like to take the liberty of inviting myself to come and have lunch with you.'

"Then he left and returned to his ship; the next morning he put one of the ship's cats up the sleeve of his gown and went to lunch with the King. When he arrived, before lunch was served, he was given a stick; he sat down, and as the bread and the victuals were brought to the table, there rushed in a multitude of mice. At that point the master of the ship unfastened his sleeve. The cat jumped out and began to fight those mice, and in no time it killed over one hundred of them. All the others fled, wild with fear.

"The King and all those who were present thought that that was an extraordinary thing, and they did not believe it possible that such a small animal could be so fierce and so nimble. The King wanted to know all about cats: where they were born, where they found their food, and what they ate. The merchant told him, and then he said:

" 'Fine Sire, I wish to make you a present of twenty-two pairs of these cats; if you have them properly cared for, in a few years your whole kingdom will be full of them.'

"The King found his gift so wonderful and fine that he thought he would never be able to reward him as he deserved. He asked for the advice of his wise men on what kind of appropriate recompense he should give the merchant; and since he was responsible for the salvation of his whole realm, he decided to give him over two hundred thousand ducats' worth of gold, silver, and jewels. Then the merchant took fond leave of the king and returned to Genoa with his ships.

"Within a few days the news of his immense wealth and of how good fortune had brought him such a large treasure spread far and wide. Everybody was astonished and stunned; and in spite of the incredibly long, unusual and dangerous voyage, many thought of going to that island and bringing it a large number of similar animals.

"Among the many was one man who was more courageous than the others, but not wise. He was more rash than all the others; and, paying no attention to the advice of the one who had returned from there, he decided to do things his own way: that is, to take along much more valuable things than cats in order to receive a greater reward. He went and took to the King fine clothes of gold and silver brocade, bedspreads, ornaments for horses, dogs, and birds, as well as many manufactured items and expensive clothes, for a total value of over thirteen thousand ducats.

"After a long time, and after having encountered very great dangers, his ship landed safely at the abovementioned island, where he presented the King with his expensive gifts. The King happily accepted them and honored him with banquets, and in other ways.

"When the merchant took leave, the King consulted his wise men on what he should give him: some said the King should give him two hundred thousand ducats, others jewels, others other things. But the King felt that all that wouldn't be enough; and since he was a most generous and magnanimous king, he concluded that he should give him part of his most valued and treasured possessions. Thus he gave him two of his cats; and the poor, unfortunate merchant returned to Genoa utterly heartbroken.

"That is exactly what I wanted to tell you: you refused to take my advice, and out of greed and envy you precipitatedly dashed into a business that was entirely unknown to you. You insisted on going along, and now see what happened to you; you will never get half of your money back."

## 18

### *Reply to certain women who were speaking ill of Arlotto's family*

DURING the summer, when it is hot, it is an old custom with our Florentine women to gather after lunch
until practically supper time in some courtyard or in
front of their doorsteps, where most of the time they
do their chores, such as spinning or sewing.

One evening at vespers, Priest Arlotto was passing
through Borgo Santo Apostolo and ran into a group of
women who were sewing on a doorstep. One of the
women addressed him:

"Father, much good may it do you! Your relative
Corrado had a beautiful baby boy. He certainly is a
much better man than most, for at seventy years of age
he has been able to do what many a young man of twenty
cannot. Thanks to his beautiful wife, of course!"

Priest Arlotto realized two things: they were scoff-
ing at him, and they were suggesting that his relative
was a cuckold and his wife a harlot, whereas she
was a fine, honest, and very beautiful young woman of
noble blood. He reacted immediately, and without
thinking said:

"Do you believe that there are no other whores besides yourselves?"

## 19

### *Arlotto plays a trick on Canon Rosello from Arezzo who was Papal Collector in France*

ON his way back from France, Master Rosello [9]
stopped only a short while in Florence because a plague

epidemic was ravaging that city. On the following morning he decided to move on to Arezzo; and, fearful that it might not be safe to stop along the way, he resolved to spend the night with a priest friend of his who lived a short distance beyond the bridge at Levane, where he had a poor church with an income of about twenty ducats a year.

As he was riding through the market at Figline, he bought four capons and seven partridges; and in the afternoon he arrived at Levane with his entourage of about sixteen people, twelve horses, eight dogs and two birds. They dismounted from their horses and knocked at the door. Priest Arlotto came to open it; and after the customary greetings, Master Rossello said:

"Where is the priest of this church, and what are you doing here?"

Priest Arlotto replied: "The priest went to the Casentino to settle a quarrel over a murder case; he left this morning and he will be gone two days. I am here because of the plague that, as you have probably heard, is laying waste Florence and our towns. Now I am watching over this house."

Master Rosello said: "Since he is not here, I am just as happy to see you here."

When Priest Arlotto saw the capons and the partridges, he had the horses unsaddled and taken into the stables. Then he had the capons and partridges plucked and put into a large pot on the fire: he had them boiled so that they wouldn't be so easily carried off as if they were roasted. The Priest was quite indignant, and he said to himself: "Just look at how indiscreet that fellow is; he comes into the house of a poor priest who has hardly one hundred lire of income a year, and he brings along such a crowd of men and horses. There must be thirty of them!" And forthwith, he worked out a plan as to what he should do. He called in a mischievous altar boy and told him what to say in case he were asked any questions; and further that when he gave him a certain sign, he should toll the church bell three times for the dead. Then he took Master Rosello by the arm and led him for a stroll through the property. After he had shown him the church, which had been repaired, whitewashed and reroofed, he took him through the vineyard. While they were inspecting the seedlings and the olive trees, Priest Arlotto had nothing but high praise for the priest and said to Master Rosello:

"That priest works wonders; I am really amazed that he has been able to accomplish so much with his paltry income." And as he was saying this the altar boy began tolling vigorously for the dead.

"Father, what's that?" Master Rosello said.

And he replied: "Nothing at all."

At the same time, the Priest held on firmly to Master Rosello's arm. They resumed their conversation, and again the church bell rang a full peal. Master Rosello grew pale, and asked Priest Arlotto again: "What's the meaning of that tolling?"

"It's nothing of much importance. A little seven-year-old boy died. Thank Heaven things have improved: last week nine people died, and this week only three so far."

Master Rosello, who was walking arm in arm with the Priest, grew deadly pale and scampered away without asking any more questions. He hastily assembled his attendants, had the horses saddled and bridled, and without saying anything else, betook himself to Quarata, which is three miles away from Arezzo. He came to the inn and knocked at the door. The innkeeper got out of bed in great amazement, and said:

"Why did you get here so late? It's nearly eleven. Did you meet with some mishap on the way?"

As a result of much fear, fatigue of riding through

the night, hunger, and lack of sleep, Master Rosello was on the verge of fainting; but as soon as he was able to speak, he told the innkeeper the whole story.

The innkeeper replied and said: "Undoubtedly, Master Rosello, this was a jest; for I can assure you that from here as far as the Incisa, and from here down as far as Rome, there hasn't even been a headache!"

Master Rosello said: "This is a typical jest of Priest Arlotto's; what bothers me most is that we left four capons and seven partridges at his place."

Then one of his attendants said: "That's not all; because of your fear and your haste, we also left there two halters, a blacksmith's leather pouch with some tools, and a hat."

Master Rosello said: "What is even worse is the fact that we will never get anything back, for whatever is left in the house of a priest is more irretrievably lost than if it had been dropped in the middle of the sea."

Priest Arlotto, for his part, could not refrain from rebuking Master Rosello, and he sent him a letter to Arezzo in which he told him about his indiscretion in coming to seek lodgings with such a large retinue at the house of a poor priest.

When the priest returned from the Casentino, he and Priest Arlotto enjoyed the partridges and the four capons in honor of Master Rosello.

20

*Ten talented astronomers who went mad*

❦ CERTAIN learned and upright citizens were taking a stroll about two miles outside of Florence when in a field behind a house they ran into several boon companions who were jousting on horseback with reeds; among these was Priest Arlotto.

Priest Arlotto felt somewhat ashamed to be seen, carrying on in that manner, by those honorable men, who greeted him and said: "What are you doing there with that reed in your hand?"

"We had lunch in that house yonder," he replied, "and perhaps guzzled too heavily, and it is quite possible that now we are either completely drunk or somewhat intoxicated! What is happening to me reminds me of what happened to ten good astronomers: through science and their knowledge of astrology, they saw that in their town on a certain day it would rain in such an extraordinary fashion that the thoroughly drenched earth would let out such a stench that all those exposed to it—men and women, adults and children—would go mad. This was to be the result of a long period of drought and of the parched condition of the soil.

"Those astronomers comforted one another and said: 'When the whole population will go mad, since we will not be exposed to the stench and will not be affected by it, we will become the masters of the town.'

"The prognosticated day for the heavy rains arrived. Without saying anything to the people, those astronomers locked all the doors and the windows of their houses very tightly, so that when it rained, they did not smell the stench. The whole population, on the other hand, on account of that awful stench turned mad; and, as long as they could stand up, they danced and laughed.

"When the rain stopped and the stench died away, the astronomers came out; and as the people saw them they rushed toward them. It turned out that, in order not to be chased out of town or killed, the astronomers found it necessary to behave as crazily as the rest of the population.

"Now I find myself in the identical predicament as

those astronomers; therefore, I beg you in the name of God to overlook my foolish behavior."

## 21

### *Witty reply of Priest Arlotto to a stingy friend*

ONE of Priest Arlotto's friends, but not a member of any epicurean club, was very stingy. One morning during Lent he invited our Priest for lunch. Priest Arlotto accepted and went to his house. After they were seated at the table, they were served large bowls of chick-pea soup; but the soup was very watery and poorly seasoned with olive oil. There were so few chick-peas floating about in the bowl that the Priest was unable to spear a single one—either with his fork or with the tip of his knife—nor was he successful in seizing any of them with his hands.

Then he began unfastening his belt and unbuttoning his coat. One of the guests said to him:

"What on earth are you doing, Father?"

And he replied: "Can't you see, you ox? I am getting undressed so that I can dive into this bowl, since there is no other way of getting to those chick-peas; and I intend to eat a few of them this morning."

## 22

### *The dry pumpkin*

PRIEST ARLOTTO decided to see how many good days there are in one year. He took a dry pumpkin and made a hole in it; and when someone invited him to lunch or dinner and he had a good time, he considered that day a good one, and he put a bean into the pumpkin. If on a certain day he earned ten or twenty *soldi*,[10] he thought that that day was also a good one, and he slipped another bean into the pumpkin.

One day he lost a wallet in which he had twenty *soldi;* then the Priest took the pumpkin and removed one bean from it.

He followed that practice until the last day of the year: then he counted all the beans he had left in the pumpkin: thus he was able to tell how many good days he had had during the year.

### 23

### *Reply to a peasant who*
### *was angry at Priest Arlotto*

℘ PRIEST ARLOTTO asked a peasant named Nicolò di Bardoccio to go and work in his orchard the following day. He wanted him to arrive on the job early in the morning, and he told him three times: "Come tomorrow morning early." Nicolò replied:

"Father, you don't have to tell me again; without fail I shall be there at such and such a time. I'll be the first workman on the job, unless I drop dead. If I do not show up, you may be sure I'll be dead."

The next morning the other workmen had been in the orchard about two hours, and it was already past nine o'clock; Nicolò was nowhere to be seen. Priest Arlotto then went into the church and rang a full peal for the dead. Several people came into the church and asked him:

"Who died?"

And the Priest replied: "Nicolò di Bardoccio died."

They all marveled at this, and some said: "I saw him last night and he seemed hale and hardy."

While they were commenting on this, Nicolò arrived on the scene with a spade on his shoulder; and he said angrily to the Priest: "What in tarnation have you done? All my relatives rushed to my house weeping over my death."

"Didn't you tell me, 'If I don't come early, you may be sure I'm dead'? I thought that you could read the future and that you knew it and that you had actually died. That's why I tolled the bell; I thought you would appreciate it."

## 24

### *The wind had blown the memos into the sea*

EVERYBODY knew that Priest Arlotto was all set to sail to Flanders on the flagship, and many of his friends had asked favors of him. Some of them had written their order for two tapestries on a piece of paper so that he would not forget, and they had given him twelve or fifteen ducats, saying: "If this shouldn't be enough, we will reimburse you when you return; we shall pay you for your trouble, and we will be very grateful to you."

Some ungrateful individuals had given him a memorandum for one hundred pounds of tin or brass, but they had given him no money. They had merely said: "We shall pay you when you come back."

The galleys set sail; and when Priest Arlotto saw that they were only a few hours way from the coast of Flanders, he said: "I think I'd better straighten out my bags." He found the memos he had been given, and he set them on the railing of the ship; then he placed the money on the orders he had been given. He had just put down the last handful of coins when a gust of wind blew the orders for which he had not been given any money into the sea. The orders that were weighed down by the coins did not budge.

Priest Arlotto put everything back in place. When the ship landed, he went to Bruges; and eventually he made the purchases.

When he returned to Florence, his friends came to him and said: "Did you buy the tapestries for us?"

"Yes," said the Priest. "I spent about fifteen ducats, and you gave me fourteen." They gave him the balance, and they thanked him.

Another group of people went to see him and asked: "Father, did you buy the brass and the tin for us?"

The Priest said: "I met with a mishap; I was spreading out a few trifles of mine on the railing of the galley, and with them the pieces of paper on which you had scribbled your orders. Since those notes of yours were so light, they were blown into the sea; thus, I was unable to buy what you wanted, because I could not recall what you wanted."

They replied: "How is it then that you brought the tapestries for the others?"

And the Priest said: "It's very simple. Since their notes were weighed down by the money they had given me in advance, nothing happened to them. Yours, on the other hand, had nothing to hold them down; and when a gust of wind came up unexpectedly, they were blown away."


## 25

### Priest Arlotto deceives the customs officers

THE FLORENTINE galleys, on one of which was our Priest, were at anchor at L'Ecluse—the port of Bruges —and were about to set sail to return to Florence. As

was customary, one of the officers of the Duke of
Burgundy came to search the galleys to see whether
there were any goods that were being smuggled out of
the country, for which no export duty had been paid.

Priest Arlotto heard that this search was about to
be carried out on the galley on which he was traveling.
Since in his cabin he had a certain amount of tin, linen,
and woolen cloths on which he had not paid the customs tax, he hastily went down to his cabin; he washed
his face with water in which he had dissolved a pinch
of saffron; he wrapped his loose overcoat around his
body and his head and lay down on his cot right next
to the above-mentioned goods.

When the officer came into his cabin, the Priest began moaning loudly. The officer asked him: "What's
the matter with you, sir?"

Priest Arlotto replied in a sorrowful tone: "Woe is
me! I am running a high fever, and I should like either
a barber or a physician to cut open a swelling I have in
my groin."

The officer surmised that he had the plague and got
off the galley as quickly as he could without carrying
out his search.

## 26

### *Why Priest Arlotto puffed when he washed his face*

℧ PRIEST ARLOTTO was asked by an idler why he puffed and made a lot of noise with his mouth when he washed his face. He replied:

"So that when I wash my face you may not think that I am washing my behind, for in each case I use a different method."

## 27

### *Priest Arlotto teaches a thief a lesson*

℧ ON VARIOUS occasions Priest Arlotto discovered that someone had stolen the eggs from the nests of his chickens. He was determined to discover the thief, and he told his farmer to be on the lookout. One day his farmer told him: "The man who has been stealing your eggs is your farm hand. He just stole one dozen of them, and he is carrying them under his shirt."

As everyone knows, peasants wear a shirt that is open in front; and they hold up their trousers with a sash or a rope, so that their shirt puffs out above the waist. That's where this fellow put the eggs, and he had been carrying out his little scheme at least twice a week.

When the peasant got as far as the door on his way out, Priest Arlotto came up to him and asked him to have lunch with him. He refused, saying: "I must go home, first; I'll be right back."

"Come now; don't leave me here alone," the Priest said. Pretending to coax him, he put his arms around him and hugged him, continuing, "Come now, I don't want you to leave me; let's go drink a glass of wine together."

And he kept on hugging him tightly, so that all the eggs were broken, and began dripping down his thighs and legs.

## 28

### *The poor yield of Priest Arlotto's plot*

ONE year among others, the harvest of grain and fruit was excellent all over Italy and Tuscany, especially in the countryside around Florence. Everybody was rejoicing and talking about the large harvest of his land.

One day Priest Arlotto was with a group of men who were talking about their good luck; and after he had listened to them for a while, he said:

"I had a completely different experience from yours; I can assure you that my best plot of land gave me a very poor crop."

All the men who were in Arlotto's company were amazed and asked him how that could be possible, and what plot he was talking about that had produced such poor crop.

"It is the cemetery back of my church," he replied. "Every year it gives me an income of from about fifty to sixty lire, because every year I usually bury there from six to eight people; and for each body, which takes up three yards of land, I get ten lire. This year my cemetery hasn't produced anything at all because as yet no one has died, and that grieves me a great deal."

## 29
### *The woodcutters who grunted*

℘ AS he often did, Priest Arlotto went one day to spend a few hours with Father Antonio, who was the parish priest of the church of Cercina.[11] He found that Father Antonio was having some large logs split and cut by three woodcutters; and he noticed that every time those workmen brought the axe down on the logs, they let out a guttural grunt: "Heh, heh!" Just like the pepper-pounders in Venice, who, every time they bring down the heavy pestles into the mortar, utter a certain guttural sound: "Haoh, haoh!"

Priest Arlotto made the priest of Cercina believe that every time his workmen uttered that grunt, they wasted a lot of precious time. The priest of Cercina, who swallowed what Priest Arlotto told him, said: "What can I do about it?"

"You should hire a hand to grunt for them."

The priest of Cercina, who was stingy, said: "I don't want to hire another hand today."

Priest Arlotto replied: "I get you! You want me to work for my lunch and dinner today. All right, then; I will do it, and they will be able to work faster." And he said to the woodcutters:

"I'll grunt for you; you just keep on splitting and cutting. If I should have to go pass some water, you will stop working and wait for me to come back."

At that point, Father Antonio went on certain errands of his and did not return until evening. As soon as the priest of Cercina left, Priest Arlotto left also; and the woodcutters stopped working.

Late in the afternoon the priest of Cercina came to see how much work the woodcutters had done and found that they were standing around idly and had done practically nothing from the time he had left. He immediately began shouting and swearing at them because they were not working.

"It is your fault," the woodcutters said. "You told us not to grunt anymore because Priest Arlotto would go 'Heh, heh' for us. As soon as you left, he left also; he said that he was going to pass some water and that he would be right back. We stopped working, and we have been waiting for him. You see that it is your fault and his fault too. We did what we were told to do."

The priest of Cercina said: "This is one of his jokes. Priest Arlotto would die if he were to let a single day go by without playing some trick."

## 30

### *Priest Arlotto goes to the feast at Cercina*

EVERY year, on the occurrence of the feast of the patron saint of Cercina, Father Antonio of Cercina held a beautiful feast. On that day, large numbers of devoted people—priests and laymen—came from Florence and other towns; and on that day, many people, especially farmers, brought Father Antonio numerous gifts.

One particular year the feast was attended by many good laymen and clergymen, among whom was the Archbishop of Florence. On that occasion, Priest Arlotto was in charge of the luncheon and the dinner to which many guests were invited.

After lunch, while Priest Arlotto was conversing with the Archbishop, the cook came up to him and whispered into his ear:

"A man brought four capons; how shall I cook them?"

"Roast them," the Priest whispered back.

Shortly afterwards the cook returned and said: "A man brought nearly twenty pounds of fish."

"Fry them."

Thus, during his conversation with the Archbishop, the cook came to him several times, finally saying: "Someone brought two young goats; how should I fix them?"

Priest Arlotto became infuriated at the foolish cook and turned to him and said loudly:

"Get out of here, and don't you dare come back to ask me any more questions. If Christ himself is brought to you, roast him!"

## 31
### *A peasant wondered whether he should observe a holiday*

A SIMPLE-HEARTED poor man came to see Priest Arlotto on the morning of the feast of St. Luke the Evangelist. He greeted him, and then he asked: "Father, is this a feast of obligation?"

Considering his simplicity and poverty, the Priest asked him: "Do you have any bread in your house?"

"No, Father."

Then Priest Arlotto said: "Go ahead and work, for today is not a feast of obligation for you."

## 32
### *Priest Arlotto teaches a mouse to hunt mice*

WHEN PRIEST ARLOTTO returned from overseas and went to his house next to the church, he found that during his absence of nearly thirteen months, mice had gnawed a good part of his household furniture and had ruined two mattresses and several pieces of woolen and linen cloths. He was quite upset about this and said to the mice: "I will never feel that I have taken my revenge on you until one of you turns into a cat, and all of you are exterminated."

He worked out a plan; and by means of traps and other devices, he caught most of the mice alive and locked them up in a large old barrel, which he no longer used. He left them there for a month. During that time, he often went to look into the barrel and noticed that the mice were eating one another out of hunger. This went on until only one mouse was left alive; he hung a bell around his neck and let him loose around the house, and he said to him:

"I want to see what you can do."

Since that mouse had fed on the other mice for a whole month, it hunted about the house like a cat and ate all the mice it caught. It lived for a while after that; and during the next three years, Priest Arlotto never saw a mouse in his house except the one with the bell; because the other mice scampered away when they heard the bell. Furthermore, the belled mouse devoured all the mice it could catch. Thus, the house of Priest Arlotto was free of mice for nearly three years; then the belled mouse died, and Priest Arlotto grieved over its death.

## 33
### *Morning prayers*

❧ "WHAT prayer do you recommend that I say in the morning, so that it will avail me?" a man asked Priest Arlotto.

He replied: "When you rise, make the sign of the

holy cross and say devotedly a Hail Father and a Hail Mary, and then say these words: 'My Lord Jesus Christ, protect me from the fury and the hands of peasants, from the conscience of priests, from doctors' prescriptions, from the so-ons and so-forths of lawyers, from a man who hears two Masses every morning, and from those who always say "On my word of honor." ' "

## 34
### *The thrushes were better than the sausage*

ONE evening Priest Arlotto was having supper in a farmhouse with a group of upright men. It began raining; and everyone was rejoicing and praising the rain, for it hadn't rained for a long time. They were saying:

"It will be good for the wheat and the fodder and excellent for the wine."

Noticing that at the table no one was adding a single drop of water to his wine, Priest Arlotto said:

"You praise to the sky the wonderful properties of water, and yet not one of you drinks any of it."

At that same supper, a plateful of thrushes and a plateful of sausage were placed on the table. Priest Arlotto tasted a piece of sausage and began giving it high praises, saying that he had never eaten better sausage, so that everyone began eating it. Meanwhile, Priest Arlotto ate the fattest and best thrushes on the plate. When the others had finished the sausage and turned to the other plate, they discovered that the Priest had eaten the best thrushes; and they said to him:

"You praised the sausage so much, and yet you concentrated on the thrushes. How's that?"

Priest Arlotto replied: "It is true that I said that the sausage was very good, but the thrushes were better;

and so I followed your example, for you praised water and drank unadulterated wine."

## 35
### *The cuckoo had sung for Priest Arlotto*

❧ TWO peasants came to Priest Arlotto and said: "We were hoeing in a vineyard when we heard the cuckoo sing. Each one of us said, 'He sang for me.' [12] Now there is great disagreement between us. We have made a bet: one of us has put up a donkey worth twenty lire; the other has put up money. We have agreed to ask for your opinion and to abide by your judgment."

Priest Arlotto accepted, and the two peasants left. That evening one of them went secretly to see the Priest and brought him two small cheeses in order to bribe him. The Priest told him not to worry. The peasant had hardly left when the other peasant went to Priest Arlotto's house and brought him twenty eggs; and, like the first, he begged him to take his side.

The next morning the one who had brought the cheeses came and brought two hens and entreated the Priest once more. After he left, the peasant who had brought the eggs came and begged him while handing him two capons. Thus, they called on Priest Arlotto several times, and each present they brought was better than the previous one.

After Priest Arlotto had received many gifts, he called in the two peasants and said to them:

"I want to save your bets, namely your donkey and your twenty lire, because I have come to the conclusion that the cuckoo sang for me and not for either of you. And to prove to you that I have judged rightly, you know that each one of you has brought me five or six gifts. I would return them to you, great fools that you

are; but I realize that if you had made this arrange-
ment with someone else, you wouldn't get them back.
Next time use your heads; now, as long as your gifts
last, come and enjoy them with me."


## 36

### *Shrewd reply to a peasant*
### *who wanted some wheat*

A PEASANT came to Priest Arlotto and said, "I'd
like you to lend me a sackful of wheat."

The priest replied: "Gladly! Take your sack; go
down to the far corner of the basement where you got
it last year, and fill your sack."

The peasant went, and then he said to the Priest, "I
looked all around the same end of the basement as last
year, but I could find neither wheat nor fodder."

"Didn't you find the wheat I lent you last year?"

"No, Father."

"Well," the Priest said, "you mustn't have returned
the wheat I lent you last year; if you had returned it,
now I could lend you some again."


## 37

### *Priest Arlotto blesses some jokers with oil*

A GROUP of honorable citizens called on Priest Arlotto, and he received them in his usual hospitable
manner.

At lunch time, Priest Arlotto went on an errand in
the neighborhood; and since he was delayed somewhat, his guests lost their patience: they locked the
Priest out of the house and ate not only their portions,
but his as well. Then they opened the door, and Priest

Arlotto went in; he laughed at the whole thing and lunched on bread and cheese.

After lunch Priest Arlotto went into the church and filled the stoup with holy water and oil. When his guests came into the church, he sang a psalm of thanks to God; and when he gave them the holy water for the sign of the cross, he fixed their clothes as they deserved. They laughed at the joke they had played on the Priest and didn't notice until the following day that their gowns were covered with oil spots.

## 38

### *Priest Arlotto writes his own epitaph*

BEFORE his death Priest Arlotto had two tombs made: one in the church of his parish, and the other in the Priests' Hospital in Florence. Since he was a most charitable man, he wanted to be as generous with his possessions in death, as he had been during his life.

He himself wrote his own epitaph for his tomb in his parish church: I am not sure how it read, because I have not been in that church since he had his tomb built.

On his tomb in Florence he had these words written in Italian:

† † †

QUESTA SIPOLTURA HA FATTO FARE EL PIOVANO ARLOTTO PER SE E PER TUTTE QUELLE PERSONE LE QUALI VI VOLESSINO DRENTO ENTRARE

† † †

["Priest Arlotto had this tomb made for himself and for all those who might wish to enter it"]

# IV

## Angelo Poliziano

### 1454-1494

# POLIZIANO

Angelo Poliziano got his surname from the Tuscan town in which he was born: Montepulciano [*Mons Politianus*, in Latin]. When his father was killed in 1464, his mother sent him to a relative in Florence. There, Angelo studied under the great humanists of the time; and he soon passed under the protection of Lorenzo de' Medici, who had learned of his brilliant mind. In 1475 Poliziano was entrusted with the education of Lorenzo's son Piero. Owing to misunderstandings with the boy's mother, Clarice, he left Florence and went to the court of the Gonzagas in Mantua; but he was called back to Florence the same year (1480), and until his death he taught Greek and Latin letters at the *Studio*, or university.

Poliziano was a close friend of the various members of the Medici circle and one of the most learned scholars of his time. He wrote numerous works in both Latin and Italian. The best known of his Italian works are the *Orfeo*, a charming, poetical version of the legend of Orpheus and Eurydice; *Le stanze per la giostra*, an unfinished poem in honor of a tournament that was held in Florence, and won by Lorenzo's younger brother Giuliano; and numerous short poems that go under the title of *Ballate e rispetti*.

It has been now definitely proved by Albert Wesselski,[1] and more recently by Gianfranco Folena,[2] that Poliziano was the author of a group of 413 anecdotes and proverbs (the latter are in the minority). This is by far the most original collection of fifteenth-century anecdotes in the Italian language. It is known by the

title given it by Ludovico Domenichi, *Bel libretto,*
"Beautiful little book"; and it contains the witticisms,
repartees, and anecdotes that Poliziano jotted down
day by day during his last years as a member of the
Medici household (1477–1479). To date, this work
of Poliziano, which was lent to Domenichi by a friend
toward the middle of the sixteenth century and then
was mysteriously lost, was, either completely or with
but a few omissions, published by Domenichi as part of
his first book of facetiae in 1548, and several years ago
with an introduction and notes by Albert Wesselski
with the title *Angelo Polizianos Tagebuch,* "Angelo
Poliziano's Diary."

Contrary to the stories we have met in Bracciolini
and Arlotto, Poliziano's are very short and pungent.
The sole interest in Poliziano's mind seems to have
been the lightning-quick repartee. There is no effort
at style in this work of a great stylist. In some of the
instances we find mere notes, such as one jots down
after hearing a good story in order to be able to recall
it later. As it has come down to us, this work of Poliziano definitely was not meant for publication; some of
the anecdotes he recorded about certain contemporaries
of his might have cut to the quick the families involved!

A few of Poliziano's anecdotes betray traditional
elements; but most of them are original, and they are
of great interest because they are about the writer's
contemporaries or near-contemporaries—Cosimo de'
Medici, Lorenzo de' Medici, Nannina de' Medici,
Donatello, Luigi Pulci, Pope Sixtus IV, Francesco
Sforza, Palla Strozzi, Sandro Botticelli, Marsilio
Ficino, and so on and so on.

## I
### *Why priests can kick and get away with it*

LORENZO DE' MEDICI was with a group of people who were talking about priests, and someone said that one cannot protect himself from them; thereupon Lorenzo said that it is no wonder; for, since they wear long cassocks, they can give a kick before one can see their leg move.

## 2
### *Fools are like kidneys*

COSIMO DE' MEDICI used to say that Francesco Sacchetti,[3] who always associated with learned men but did not know anything, was like the kidney—which is always surrounded by fat but stays lean.

## 3
### *Of a very fat man*

WHILE Martino dello Scarfa, who was very fat and had a large belly, was urinating one day, he saw that a boy was staring at him; he turned to him and said: "If you see him, say hello to him for me, for I haven't seen him in ten years."

## 4
### *The room without a view*

A FELLOW was complaining that a column blocked his view from one of his windows. Strozzo said to him: "There is a good remedy for that."

That fellow asked him: "What?"
He replied: "Wall up the window."

## 5
### *Witticism at a hanging*

೪ IN THE city of Prato messer Giorgio Ginori was
hanging with his own hands a man who had committed
a crime against the State. When the latter asked him,
"Please, let me recite a Hail Mary first!", messer
Giorgio said pushing him off: "Jump down, you will
say it later!"

## 6
### *Artistic rivalry*

೪ THE sculptor Mino [da Fiesole], who was making
a statue of St. Paul for Pope Paul, made it so thin that
he ruined it. The Pope was very angry; and when he
told messer Battista Alberti [4] about it, the latter said
that Mino had not made a mistake: for this was the
best thing he had ever done.

## 7
### *Donatello and the statue of Gattamelata*

೪ DONATELLO was making a bronze statue of Captain
Gattamelata; [5] and since he was constantly goaded to
hurry with it, he took a hammer and crushed the head
of the statue. When the Signori of Venice heard about
this, they asked him to come in and, among other
threats, they told him that they would bash his head in
just as he had done to the statue.

Donatello: "It's all right with me, as long as you feel that you will be able to do my head over as I will do your Captain's."

## 8

### *Cosimo de' Medici and the peasant*

℘ COSIMO DE' MEDICI had some Anjou pears placed before a peasant to whom breakfast was being served. It happened that, since the latter was accustomed to eating only little wild pears, he said: "Well, we feed these to the hogs!"

Turning to a waiter, Cosimo said: "We certainly don't; take them away!"

## 9

### *Dreams can be worth more than reality*

℘ UPON being asked by Ugolino Martelli why he got up late in the morning, Lorenzo de' Medici in turn asked him what he had done early that morning; and when he recounted a few inconsequential things he had done, Lorenzo said: "What I was dreaming of at that time was worth more than what you were doing."

## 10

### *Witty remark of Dante*

℘ DANTE was once having lunch with a man who had become so heated up by his constant talking and by the wine he had been drinking, that he was perspiring profusely. When, in connection with something he had said, he stated appropriately that "He who speaks the truth does not strain himself," Dante replied: "I was wondering why you were perspiring so much!"

## 11
### The old coat with a new patch

A POOR man was wearing a gray coat that had a patch of fine silk cloth. Upon being derided for it, he said: "I wish the rest of the coat were like it!"

## 12
### The large cabbage and the huge cauldron

TWO fellows were vying with each other in telling the wonderful things they had seen. One of them said that in a certain land he had seen a cabbage that was so large that fifteen hundred men on horseback had gathered under it.

The other said: "I saw in a land a cauldron that was being built by one hundred workmen; and it was so large that they could not hear one another, so far were they one from the other."

The first fellow asked: "What on earth did they want to do with such a large cauldron?"

He replied, "Cook that cabbage!"

## 13
### The preacher who never sent anyone to Hell

AS some people were saying that Father Antonio Schiattesi, who was a fat preacher, never sent anyone to Hell, one of them said: "He is doing the right thing; for, since he expects to go there himself, he knows that no one else would fit."

Another added: "Indeed, he does it so that he will not be recognized by the ones whom he is admonishing!"

## 14
### *A biting retort by Dante*

℘ DANTE asked a peasant what time it was, and he replied rudely: "It's the time when beasts go to drink."

Whereupon Dante said to him: "Then, what are you doing here?"

## 15
### *Ask me no questions . . .*

℘ MESSER Antonio da Cercina was asking a peasant who was coming from Florence, "What's going on in Florence? What do they say? Tell us a few lies."

He replied, "They say that you are a good man."

## 16
### *The cross-eyed student*

℘ AS Lorenzo de' Medici was returning from Pisa, he saw a cross-eyed student. He turned to his companions and said, "He will be the most learned man of this university." Being asked why, he replied, "Because he will read at the same time both pages of a book."

## 17
### *The hen cannot hatch away from the nest*

℘ WHEN messer Rinaldo degli Albizzi was exiled from Florence with others, he sent word to Cosimo [de' Medici] that the hen was hatching [revenge]. Cosimo replied that the hen could hardly hatch, since she was away from the nest.

## 18

### *Fools are the happiest of people*

❦ THEY say that the above messer Rinaldo once lost his mind. There was a simple woman who had a son who had gone crazy; and as she was inquiring of some people what remedy there was to cure him, they referred her to the mentioned messer Rinaldo. The woman found him and said to him: "Messer Rinaldo, I heard that once you went out of your mind; and therefore I beg you to tell me how you got cured; for I have a son who has gone crazy."

Realizing how simple-minded that woman was, he replied: "For goodness' sake don't do anything about it, my good lady; for I never had such a wonderful time as when I was crazy!"

## 19

### *The difference between a wise woman*
### *and a foolish one*

❦ MESSER BARTOLOMEO, a physician from Pistoia, was a very singular man. When he was looking for a wife, two women were brought before him; one had a meager dowry but was a wise woman; the other was not very wise but had three hundred ducats of dowry more than the first. Messer Bartolomeo observed that between the craziest and the wisest woman in the world there wasn't a grain of bird-seed difference and that he did not want to pay three hundred ducats for that grain.

## 20

### Why messer Bartolomeo
### took a wife in his old age

❧ THE above-mentioned Bartolomeo was asked why in his old age he had gotten married. He replied that old people lose their common sense and that in his youth, when he had his wits about him, he had been on his guard against getting married; but that when he had grown old, being less wise, he had been trapped.

## 21

### Why one should marry a small woman

❧ WHEN a relative of messer Bartolomeo from Pistoia married a small, thin woman, the said messer Bartolomeo commended him; for, he said, according to him, of women the less one takes, the better off one is.

## 22

### A dig at the Florentines

❧ WHEN one day a group of people from Siena were saying that on a certain occasion the Florentines had lost their common sense, Cosimo said: "They couldn't possibly lose it!"

## 23

### It is not wise to tease Florentines

❧ WHEN messer Agnolo della Stufa was ambassador in Rimini, the people of Rimini found it strange that he wore a large, spacious hood, as was then customary; whereas they went out bareheaded even in January, wearing simply a scarf around their necks. And so one day, when he was in Signor Gismondo's room, a certain Marcovaldo said to him: "Messer Agnolo, your head must be very cold."

Messer Agnolo replied to him: "I'll tell you why we cover our heads in this fashion. You belong to the family of geese, which always hold their heads high on marshes and completely disregard the cold fog because they have no brains in their heads. We, on the other hand, have a brain; and since we wish to protect it, we cover it very well."

When the people around him grasped the poison that lay in the comparison, they all agreed that it is not wise to tease Florentines.


## 24
### *Witticism of Piero de' Medici*

ꙮ ON his way back from Rome, where he had been an ambassador, Piero, son of Cosimo de' Medici, visited the Signori of Perugia. It so happened that one of those Signori, who was a blockhead, said many foolish things; another Signore, in the way of a facetious apology, said to Piero: "You will have to bear with him, Piero, for you must have people like him in Florence also."

Piero retorted: "We do indeed, but we do not employ them in such positions."

## 25

### *He had no use for educated women*

℘ GIOVANNI DI BICCI, father of Cosimo [de' Medici], had a great friendship with some peasants in the mountains. Once he invited one of them to supper, and he paid him many honors; at one point he even asked his own wife Nannina to recite a few sonnets. When he asked his peasant friend what he thought of her, he praised her; but he added that he would rather have his daughters-in-law be able to make a new skirt out of two old ones than to be able to recite such fables.

## 26

### *Foresight of Cosimo de' Medici*

℘ COSIMO was being carried through his house on a chair by some of his servants [he was afflicted with the gout]. As he was about to hit against a door, he shouted; and one of his servants said to him: "What's the matter? You shout before anything happens to you!"

Cosimo replied: "Of course I shout before anything happens to me; it wouldn't do me any good after!"

## 27

### *Qualifications of a beautiful woman*

℘ HOW many things should a woman have? Three black, three white, three small, three long, three round. Namely: *black,* eye-lashes, eyes, pubic hair; *white,* hair [blonde], teeth, flesh; *small,* mouth, nose, ears; *long,* fingers, bust, neck; *round,* arms, legs, thighs.

## 28
### Justice is like water

℘ RECENTLY an old man told me that unjust things cannot last and that justice is like water that, when it is blocked along its course, either breaks through that obstruction and hindrance, or swells up and rises until it spills over the top.

## 29
### Party strife

℘ WHEN the Ciompi [6] seized the government from the Nobles, a knight of the Albizi was talking with a lowly client of his, who belonged to the Ciompi faction, and said to him: "How do you expect to rule the State with no experience, when we, who are experienced in government, were unable to do so?"

His client replied: "We will do exactly the opposite of what you did, and thus we will succeed in keeping it."

## 30
### Of a Duke who practiced astrology

℘ ONCE, when Puccio di Antonio Pucci was [a Florentine] ambassador to Duke Filippo in Milan, he had to wait a long time to get an audience with him because the said lord governed himself by the hourly conjunction of the stars. Now, when he was informed of a propitious hour by his astrologer, he sent for the said Puccio, saying that he was ready to give him an audience. But Puccio sent back word to him that he did not wish to go at that time; for, if that particular hour was favorable to the Duke, it was not favorable to him.

## 31

### *It is not the uniform that makes the soldier*

❧ [ATTENDOLO] Sforza [7] was taken out of prison by Queen Giovanna so that he might defend her State, and she made him her chief Captain. His soldiers were richly outfitted with garments and plumes. When Sforza noticed this as they were already marching, he dismounted his horse, took off his helmet, set it on a post, and began striking it with his sword, saying all along: "Defend yourself, sluggard," and thus he cut it to shreds.

His soldiers did not understand why he was doing that, so Sforza turned to them and explained that the valor of soldiers does not reside in their plumes; and to prove it to them, he pointed to the plumed helmet that was unable to defend itself.

## 32

### *The devil had not taught him that trick!*

❧ MESSER ANDREA, Prior of Lucardo, replied to one who said he had learned from him to be a hypocrite: "I did not teach you that, as that devil said." And to explain what he meant, he told this tale: "A monk, who was being compelled to fast but could not stand it, locked himself up in his cell and cooked eggs over the flame of a candle, stirring them until they were done. When the abbot saw this through a keyhole, he went in and rebuked him harshly. The monk exculpated himself, saying that a shrewd devil had taught him how to do that evil. The devil, who was hiding under the table, came out and said: 'You are lying through your teeth, for you taught me that trick!' "

## 33
### *He smiled at me, and I smiled at him*

℧ THIS saying originated with the sculptor Donatello. When a young apprentice of Donatello's with whom he had had a quarrel left him, Donatello went to see Cosimo to secure letters of introduction to the Marquis of Ferrara, where the youth had fled; and he stated to Cosimo that he wanted to go after him and kill him. Cosimo, who knew his temperament, wrote him the letters he wanted; but he secretly informed the Marquis of Donatello's nature. The Marquis granted Donatello permission to kill his apprentice on sight. However, when the youth ran into Donatello, he began smiling at him from a distance; and Donatello, who suddenly felt reconciled, smiled back at him and ran toward him. When the Marquis asked him if he had killed him, Donatello replied to him: "No, I should say not! For he smiled at me, and I smiled at him."

## 34
### *An embarrassing stain*

℧ MESSER FRANCESCO Malacarne had an oil stain on his chest, and he was irritated by the fact that everyone asked him what it was; therefore, when someone came toward him to talk to him, he would say: "Hold on, this is an oil stain; now tell me what you want."

## 35
### *The trial of Pope John*

℔ WHEN at the Council of Constance Pope John [8]
was being tried, he was listening to the accusations that
were being read against him; and after each accusation
he kept repeating: "I have done worse than that!"
Finally, upon being asked what he had done that was
worse, he replied: "When I let myself be brought here."

## 36
### *Of a lustful woman*

℔ UPON being asked which were the best rods for
women, the large, the medium or the small ones, a
woman replied: "The medium-sized ones are the best."

"Why?" she was asked.

"Because the large ones are nowhere to be found!"
she replied.

## 37
### *Of a stingy man*

℔ GERALDINO OF RIMINI, courtier of the lord,[9] was a
small and amusing man. Once he had told several stories
in the presence of many noblemen; and a certain Andrea
of Vignano, who was a well-known gentleman but very
miserly, said to him: "Geraldino, you are so amusing
that I believe nature made you so tiny for no other
reason but to make it possible for a man to carry you
in his purse and never lose you. I am planning to put

you some day in my money-purse, so that I can have you within reach at all times."

Geraldino replied: "Please don't do it, for you would never take me out of it!"

## 38
### *Witty reply of a noblewoman*

ONCE when messer Giovan Barile of Naples [10] was in Florence in the company of many gentlemen and noblewomen, Madonna Oretta of messer Geri Spini asked him what grace he would ask for, if he were to ask for one. And he replied: "That you be a diviner, because then you would know what I do not dare tell you."

She said: "Mr. Knight, he who is afraid to ask will never have the boldness to act."

## 39
### *Reply of Lorenzo de' Medici to a glutton*

LORENZO DE' MEDICI's mouth had been chapped from the cold. One morning at lunch, Butta said to him: "Lorenzo, your mouth has healed."

Lorenzo replied to him: "Yours too, because you are using it better than ever."

## 40
### *I quit! You're fired! And vice versa*

LORENZO OF Pier Francesco de' Medici [11] wanted to place a soldier at the service of a gentleman, and when the latter said, "I should be happy to employ him;

but after a while people like him always quit," Lorenzo replied: "Well, there is a good remedy for that."

The gentleman asked: "What remedy?"

And Lorenzo to him: "That you fire him before he quits."

## 41
### A boy's imagination

A FATHER said to his son, to whom he wanted to show the Court of Justice: "Do you see where those flags are? That is the Court of Justice, and the man following behind is the thief."

It happened that one day they were making an offering to St. John, and behind the pennants there came a large number of citizens. The boy remembered what his father had shown him and shouted suddenly: "Father, look at all those thieves!"

## 42
### Of a foolish preacher

A PREACHER who was delivering a sermon on the Annunciation said the following, among other stupidities: "What do you think, dear ladies, that the Virgin Mary was doing at that time? Dyeing her hair blonde? No, of course not! On the contrary! She had a crucifix before her, and she was reading the Book of Hours of Our Lady!"

## 43
### Of an overanxious boy

A LITTLE boy was riding on the croup behind his father, who was riding on the saddle; and he said naïvely: "Daddy, when you are dead, will I ride on the saddle?"

## 44
### *Of a quick-witted peasant*

A DOCTOR said to a peasant, "If you are willing to pay me one ducat, I will teach you how to litigate so that you will always win." He promised he would pay him one ducat, and the doctor said to him, "Always deny, and you will win." Then he asked him for the ducat, and the peasant immediately denied having promised it to him.

## 45
### *A foolish question deserves a foolish reply*

A CERTAIN Bernardino from Arezzo had a merry wife. Once, on a holiday, she was seated on her doorstep with her legs open; and her husband sent word to her that she should close her shop, for it was a holiday and all the stores were closed. The woman replied: "He should drop dead, because he has the key and doesn't come to lock it."

## 46
### *Witty sally of two Venetian ambassadors*

THE Venetians sent two young men as ambassadors to the Emperor, and he refused to see them. They wanted to know the reason, and they were told that it was customary to send wise men and not youths. They begged the Emperor to grant them a brief audience,

and they promised that they would not say anything
about their mission. They were received, and they spoke
thusly: "Holy Majesty, if the Signoria of Venice be-

lieved that wisdom resided in beards, they would have
sent two goats here as ambassadors."

## 47
### *Pungent reply of some Florentines*

℧ IN Rome there was a contention between Florentines and Spaniards as to which of them were the better
Christians. The Spaniards said, "We pay great honor
to the Body of Christ"; and then they became silent.

"It's no wonder," said the Florentines, "that you
pay Him a great honor; for we too, in Florence, pay
great honor to strangers."

## 48
### *Coals to Newcastle*

℧ A RICH man found a ducat. A poor man saw him
and said, "Look at that! Luck comes to you rather than
to me."

The rich man said, "You are wrong; because if you had found this ducat, you would spend it immediately and you would get rid of it. I, instead, will save it and keep it in the company of its peers."

## 49

### *Reply of Giulian Gondi*
### *to the Duke of Calabria*

DURING the war against the Florentines, the Duke of Calabria [12] said to Giulian Gondi [13] that he wouldn't remove his spurs until he had seized Florence, and the latter replied to him, "Lord, you will wear out a lot of sheets!"

## 50

### *Witty remark of Sandro Botticelli*

TO one who said, "I wish I had one hundred tongues," Sandro Botticelli said the following: "You are asking for so many tongues, and you already have one-half more than you need; why don't you ask for some brains, poor fellow, of which you have none?"

## 51

### *Women should thank mother nature*

A CERTAIN Master Agnolo Barbini said spitefully to a woman who was nursing her child, "Certainly God has bestowed upon you women a greater gift than you deserve!" And upon being asked why, he replied, "Because if He had placed your breasts between your legs as He has done to other animals, you would certainly be disgusting to see when you suckle."

# V

## Niccolò Angèli dal Bùcine

### 1448-1532?

# ANGÈLI

WE KNOW relatively little of Niccolò Angèli dal Bùcine. We know that he was born in Florence and that he must have been held in high esteem, for in 1497, he was appointed professor of humanities at the Florentine Studio; thus, he occupied the chair that a few years previously was filled by Angelo Poliziano.

The name of Niccolò remained in almost utter obscurity until the year 1874, when Giovanni Papanti published a work of his, titled *Facezie e motti dei secoli XV e XVI*, "Pleasantries and Witticisms of the XV and XVI Centuries," which was in a Florentine library in manuscript form. This booklet contains 280 pleasantries, of which 263 were assembled by Niccolò, and the remaining few—which are far less interesting—by his son Teodoro. The work of Niccolò, it seems, was compiled between 1486 and 1492.

Niccolò's work resembles in many ways the *Bel libretto* of Poliziano. Of interest to us are almost exclusively the first one hundred pleasantries, for most of the others are very similar to the corresponding ones in the *Bel libretto*. Two scholars, Albert Wesselski and Gianfranco Folena, believe that Niccolò reworked about one-third of Poliziano's facetiae.

Some of the pleasantries that Niccolò Angèli derived from Poliziano are longer than the parallels in the latter's work, and some are attributed by Niccolò to different persons.

With all this, the collection of Niccolò must be numbered among the truly important ones of the fifteenth century.

## *Of a poor man who went*
## *begging carrying a pointed iron tip*

꿈 THE Count of Tondiglia, who was the ambassador of the King of Spain to Pope Innocent VIII, was in Florence in 1486 when three ambassadors of the King of France came to Florence to win the Florentines away from the favor of King Ferrando, to inform them that the King of France intended to make an expedition against the Kingdom of Naples, and to send the Duke of Lorraine to recapture said kingdom.

When the Count of Tondiglia heard the proposal and the threats of the French messengers, he told the following pleasantry to a chancellor of Lorenzo de' Medici and to a secretary of the Signoria of Florence:

In Spain, the home of the Count of Tondiglia, there had been a poor man who went around begging with a staff that had a long, sharp iron tip; and whenever he asked someone for alms, he pointed said staff at him, as if he were ready to strike him, saying, "Say, you! Give me something for the love of God; otherwise—" As a result, many people who knew that he was crazy and troublesome, upon seeing the iron tip pointed at them and thinking that by "otherwise" he meant "I will hit you with the staff," gave him some alms in order not to have to fight him.

It so happened that one day the poor fellow made that gesture toward a spirited young knight who, as is customary in that land, carried a sword by his side. The latter became angry, seized his sword, and turning to the poor man, said: "What do you mean, otherwise?"

The poor man replied hurriedly: "Otherwise I will go on my way without money." And he departed as quickly as he could.

## 2

*It was too bad he had
drunk only one cup of wine!*

WHEN messer Giuliano Davanzati [1] was ambassador of the Florentines to the Emperor, it so happened
that on the morning that he and a fellow Florentine
were to be received by the Emperor for the first hearing, Giuliano insisted on drinking a full cup of malmsey
wine at breakfast. His companion tried to dissuade him,
saying that it was wise to go sober on such a mission.
Messer Giuliano answered, "Don't worry; it will not
have the slightest effect on me."

Indeed, messer Giuliano made his relation most
worthily; and he was highly commended by the whole
court. When they returned to their lodging, messer
Giuliano's companion threw his arms around him and
congratulated him on the honor he had won. Whereupon, messer Giuliano said to him, "Think how much
better I would have done if I had drunk more of it!"

## 3

*Had King Alfonso slept with Lady Lucretia?*

NICCOLÒ d'Andrea Giugni was ambassador of the
Florentines to King Alfonso of Naples at the time
when His Majesty was in love with Lady Lucretia, a
Neapolitan noblewoman. Out of his love for said lady,
the King had held many feasts and other entertain-
ments, always stating that he loved her for her high
qualities and that he had never sinned with her.

It so happened that one day when King Alfonso was
riding with messer Niccolò, they met Lady Lucretia

who, in a most charming and gracious manner, curt-sied to the King. Later, while talking of this lady, Niccolò said, "Your Majesty has certainly made an excellent choice in loving this lady, for she is a true paragon and mirror of beauty; but I was sorry to hear that there is a serious blemish on her body."

The King, who had been greatly pleased by the first words of Niccolò, was very much disturbed by his last statement and said immediately: "What did you hear about her?"

Giving the impression that he was loath to mention it, Niccolò said, "I have heard that she is very hairy, and that her body is covered with unusually long hair." Whereupon the King said, *Per cap de Dieu* ["By God"], it's not true."

And Niccolò countered smiling, *Per cap de Dieu, Your Majesty has slept with her!"

4

*Soldiers are like bees*

꿀 MESSER Diomede Caraffa, Count of Matalona, who was a close and intimate friend of King Ferrando of Naples, as well as his prime minister, was held to be a most wise man in his day. He used to say that soldiers are like bees, which, if they are scattered in all direc-tions, do not make honey; but if they are mustered together in a vase or in a box, they make a great deal of honey.

5

*Why Gentile degli Albizi played draughts slowly*

꿀 GENTILE degli Albizi, a Florentine citizen, often played draughts, even though he wasn't a good player.

And since on the one hand he knew that he played badly and on the other he found a great deal of pleasure in that game, he played very slowly. And when he was asked why he played so slowly, he replied that in that manner, by evening he hadn't lost very much.

### 6

*Of a friar who had asked*
*a simpleton to say "Peace"*

BROTHER Ruberto from Lecce, an observant friar of the Order of Saint Francis, as far as one can judge from the clothes, was a well-known preacher in his day. Once, in Perugia, he chose peace as his topic; he called to himself a foolish young man named Marcone, and, for a price, it was agreed that when he should ask him what he would like, Marcone was to reply "Peace." And, to this end, he instructed him as well as he could.

Later, after he had asked Marcone to take his place near the pulpit, Brother Ruberto climbed into the pulpit and began his sermon on peace. After he had spoken at length of various things, and in order to prove the necessity of peace and how it was sought by everybody and everything, he began as follows: "If you were to ask the heavens what they would like, they would say 'Peace.' The air would say, 'Peace'; the water, 'Peace'; the earth, 'Peace'; men, 'Peace'; animals, 'Peace'; plants, 'Peace.' Even fools would say 'Peace.'" And to show that it was true, he turned to Marcone and said, "And you, Marcone, what would you like?"

Marcone, who was standing next to some beautiful young women, and whose carnal instincts had been aroused to the point that he was ready for the joust, replied in a louder voice than usual, "I'd like to have one of those women!"

## 7
### Bravery of Francesco Sforza

&  WHEN the troops of Count Francesco Sforza were
camped below the walls of Piacenza, the besieged shot

a cannon and hit his horse, knocking off its rump. Whereupon Count Francesco said, *"Nondum venit hora mea"* ["My time hasn't come yet"]; and having mounted another horse forthwith, he continued on his business.

## 8

### *Why a man of thirty is not as good a husband as a younger man*

⚘ A GROUP of Florentine young men, all born of fine families, were conversing together; and to keep their discussion gay and alive, they began a debate on whether a young woman should prefer to marry a man in his thirties or one of twenty-two or less. Those who said that she should prefer a man of thirty defended their view by saying that at that age men are more serious and mature; they stay at home in the evening and spend more time with their wives. Those who gave their preference to a man of twenty-two or less said that at that age men are more passionate and make better lovers, in spite of the objection that they often go out evenings and return home late and spend less time with their wives than do men in their thirties.

This is how the debate stood when, for fun, the contestants went to ask the opinion of Monna Bartolomea, the wife of Tommaso Betti, who was an upright woman endowed with a good sense of humor. She said that in spite of the fact that the twenty-two year old men went out at night and returned home late, just the same, when they returned they were still young.

## 9

### Why the Medici's palace
### at Cafaggiuolo had a good view

GIOVANNI, son of Cosimo de' Medici, built a beautiful palace on the hillside of Fiesole. The place was barren and rocky, and it made the construction of the palace difficult; therefore, his father, Cosimo, asked him why he had chosen such a rugged terrain on which to build: clearly, the expense would be great and the profit inconsequential. His son replied that since this lot was on the hillside, he would have a view.

Cosimo said, "You couldn't find a better view than the view from Cafaggiuolo."

Since Cafaggiuolo is in the valley, Giovanni asked, "How is that possible?"

"Because," replied Cosimo, "what you can see from there belongs to you; and that is not true of Fiesole."

## 10

### Why Master Gherardo thought
### he would paint a beautiful painting

IN FLORENCE there was a painter called Gherardo, but he was not one of the best masters of his time. A man went to him to order a painting; and since he did not have much faith in Gherardo, he called on him repeatedly, showing him his sketch and asking him whether he would be able to please him. When Gherardo felt that this fellow had bothered him far too much, he pointed to a very handsome son of his who was near him and said angrily, "Do you think that this boy is beautiful?"

The man replied, "Heaven protect him, yes."

Then Gherardo added, "I made him at night in the dark; think what I can do in the daytime!"

## 11

### *Of a woman who had been raped*

ONCE a woman was seized in a soldiers' camp and was raped by about fifty pillagers. Later, during confession, she related what had happened to the priest, who told her that it was not a sin because she had been forced into submission. Whereupon the woman said, "The Lord be praised, for I finally got all I wanted without sinning!"

## 12

### *What Donatello thought of*
### *the work of a fellow sculptor*

IN the days of the excellent sculptor Donatello, there was in Florence another sculptor, Lorenzo of Bartoluccio; but he was a pale star next to that brilliant sun. This Lorenzo had sold a piece of property called Lepricino, from which he had been receiving little profit. Donatello was asked which was the best thing that the said Lorenzo had ever done; and the man who asked, of course, had in mind Lorenzo's sculptures.

Donatello replied, "Selling Lepricino."

## 13

### *Of a man who wanted to buy*
### *a wallet on credit*

℧ BERNARDO from Castiglione wanted one day to buy a wallet in Florence. He went into a shop where there was no one around except a boy who was watching it; Bernardo found a wallet he liked, and he agreed with the boy on the price—three *grossoni*. Since he didn't have any money on him, he took the wallet and said to the boy, "When I come by again, I will give you the money."

The boy took the wallet from him, put it back in its place, and, since he did not wish to give it to him on credit, said: "If you do not have any money on you, you do not need the wallet."

# VI

## *Giovanni Pontano*

### *1426-1503*

# PONTANO

GIOVANNI—or Gioviano, as he called himself—
Pontano was born at Cerreto in Umbria. He
studied at Perugia and Padua, and in 1447 he went
to the court of King Alfonso of Aragon in Naples, the
center of humanistic studies in southern Italy. He held
various posts at the Neapolitan court, and he was also
tutor of the oldest son of the King, the Duke Alfonso
of Calabria, and secretary to his learned wife, Ippolita
Sforza. Pontano was an expert diplomat, and he accompanied the Duke of Calabria on many expeditions.
In 1486, Pope Innocent VIII conferred the crown of
poet laureate on Pontano; and the following year the
Duke had him named secretary of state. His active
political life practically ceased in 1495, when the Kingdom of Naples fell into the hands of the King of France,
Charles VIII; for after the return of the Aragonese
king Ferdinand, Pontano held only minor posts. In
1498, after the death of his son, Pontano retired to
private life and spent his remaining years with his beloved books and at the Accademia Pontaniana—the
academy that had been named after him, and of which
he had been president since 1471.

Pontano was a dedicated student of classical authors
and a great Latin poet in his own right. He wrote extensively on various subjects—from astrology, which
absorbed him deeply (*Urania*), to love poetry (*Amo-
rum libri*), to pastoral poetry (*Hendecasyllabi, Lyra,*
etc.), and to conjugal love (*De amore coniugali*). Pontano was one of the greatest stylists of the fifteenth
century.

Pontano's classical training and erudition were also responsible for his work *De sermone,* which he wrote around 1499, and which deals with the art of polite and witty conversation. The most interesting and sparkling part of this treatise is that which deals with humor. Here we find numerous examples of anecdotes, facetiae, and witticisms. Pontano's stories fall into two groups: those he derived from contemporary writers and from oral tradition (including some personal recollections), and those he derived from classical authors. Pontano reveals himself a superb stylist also in the *De sermone.* His facetiae are couched in a truly literary and elegant style, and they have a closer affinity than most others with the classical apophthegm.

Because of Pontano's association with the Neapolitan court, several of his anecdotes are laid in Naples and southern Italy. A large number of Pontano's "modern" facetiae were translated by Ludovico Domenichi and included in his own large Italian collection.

# I
## Prerequisites for marital bliss

MESSER Antonio da Palermo, who was a true gentleman, was asked what was required to make a husband and wife live in harmony. Basing his opinion on
the frequency and number of arguments that constantly
arise among married couples, he said that only two
things were required: namely, that the husband be
deaf and the wife blind. Thus, the wife would not see
all the escapades of her husband, and he would not
hear his wife nagging the whole day long.

# 2
## Of a man who asked for the doctor in an inn

A FRIEND of mine who was on a journey lodged at
an inn, where he was served a supper that consisted
mainly of vegetables and some very diluted wine; and,
furthermore, he was given very little of everything.

When he had finished his supper, he wanted to send
for the doctor because he wanted to pay him. The innkeeper replied: "Sir, you are wasting your time looking
for a doctor in this town."

The gentleman went on: "Then, take an appropriate
honorarium for your services; for, feeding me as if I
were sick, you have behaved more like a doctor than
like an innkeeper."

# 3
## Of a man whose mare had been stolen

A VERY shrewd man from Cosenza complained to
a stable master that during the night his mare had been

stolen. The stable master, who had stolen the mare himself, replied to him saying he would do all he could to find her. With all that, in order to sneak the mare out of town without anyone recognizing her, he had a new saddle, a new bridle, and new trappings put on her. But the mare had not been taken far beyond the city gate when they came to a place where there was a great deal of mud. The mare slipped and in falling kicked up her legs, so that she was recognized by her master, who had chanced to get an inkling of what was going on and was lying there in wait.

He immediately went to buy a pair of drawers and returned to the stable master, saying: "Yesterday I came to beg you; now I am here to help you. Here are some drawers: you will find them very useful to guard the mares, and further they will come in handy to hide their sex."

4

*Of the Duke of Orleans who*
*praised the beauty of his homely wife*

LOUIS,[1] King of France and the father of the same Charles who a few years ago occupied with his soldiers the Kingdom of Naples, had given a daughter of his in marriage to Louis, Duke of Orleans.[2] She was homely and misshapen; and, as her husband praised her in the presence of her father by saying that she was very beautiful, the father-in-law became aware that the words of his son-in-law were somewhat pungent; therefore, in order to rebuff them, he turned the cutting edge of the sword around and said: "Add this to your praises, that your wife is the daughter of a most honest mother." For, everybody had the opinion that the mother of the Duke of Orleans had been a dishonest woman; since,

when her first husband had died, she had married a
servant of his with whom she had had relations while
her husband was still alive.

## 5

### *Of a man who had a quarrelsome wife*

 A FRIEND of mine, who is a witty and courteous
man, had a guest in his house who could not bear his
wife because she constantly quarreled with the servants
and shouted at them. He turned to his guest and said,
"Friend, I cannot understand your impatience; I have
been putting up patiently day and night with her shouts
for thirty-two years, and you cannot put up with them
for fifteen minutes!" Thus, that upright man calmed
his friend and turned his wife's anger into laughter.

## 6

### *The duckling was too small for so many gentlemen*

 PIRRINICOLO, a Gascon, had gone to an inn. When
the table was set for him, he was served a fat young
duck, which had been very well seasoned and cooked.
Just then, a Spanish wayfarer arrived; and when he
saw the fat duckling, he said: "Sir, you certainly can
welcome a friend to your table." At which Pirrinicolo
asked him his name; and he replied boldly and haugh-
tily, "My name is Alopanzio Ausimarchide Hibereneo
Alorchide."

Whereupon, Pirrinicolo added with amazement,
"How do you expect this little duckling to be enough
for four such great personages, who are Spaniards to
boot?"

## 7
### Characteristics of curly-haired men

FEDERIGO, King of Naples, had a secretary named Vito Pisanello. The latter had curly hair, just like Ethiopians usually do. It happened that King Federigo and Signor Prospero Colonna, who was the general of his army, were discussing the nature of men, and how certain physical characteristics are an indication thereof. And, as in the discussion King Federigo had said that a curly-haired man is necessarily either musically inclined or of an evil and fickle nature, Signor Prospero intervened: "Your Majesty, assuredly that Vito of yours is not musically inclined!"

## 8
### Why Marin Brancacio did not follow the King of Naples to Sicily

WHEN Charles VIII, King of France, seized the Campania district, Alfonso II, King of Naples, frightened by the savage French army, betook himself to Sicily with his son Ferrando and his brother Federigo. But Marin Brancacio [3] did not accompany them. Someone wondered about this and tried to learn the reason; whereupon, a young man of the same court, who was amiable and quick-witted, said: "Doesn't everyone know of Marino's capacity in drinking and eating and his tireless energy in having a good time? Why should he, then, be afraid of French bottles and turn his back to the dishes of those people?"

## 9

### *Why Bernardo Vitale wore glasses when he ate pike*

BERNARDO VITALE, a man of great experience and high morals, was asked by King Federigo why he put on his glasses when he ate pike. He replied, "Your Majesty is not surprised that I wear glasses when I read my friends' letters, in which there is no danger, and is surprised that I wear them when I eat such a very dangerous fish, which is full of swordlike bones each of which could easily spear my throat and kill me."

At that point a licentious youth said, "Tell me, Signor Vitale; do you wear them also when you are playing with your wife?"

"Of course," he replied, "only, then I put them on my wife's nose so that my merchandise will seem to her larger and more vigorous!"

## 10

### *The cheap flesh of a butcher's wife*

A NEAPOLITAN butcher nicknamed Rich had a very beautiful wife, who was more generous of her person than was becoming to an honest woman. For this reason, a witty fellow once said that she sold flesh [4] at a bargain price. At that point Francesco Pucci added, "No wonder, her husband is 'Rich'!"

## 11

### *The best remedy for poor eyesight*

℞ SIGNOR IACOPO SANNAZARO,[5] a noble man endowed
with a keen and witty mind, was present when, before
King Federigo, some doctors were debating what was
most beneficial to eyesight. Some said the smelling of
sweet fennel; others, the use of eyeglasses; others, various other things. Sannazaro said that the best remedy
was envy. All the doctors were quite amazed and felt
that they were being made sport of. Then, he said, "Do
you not realize that envy makes things look bigger and
fuller? And what can be more beneficial to eyes than
that which makes the sight stronger and more vigorous?" And he immediately adduced this couplet from
Ovid:

> Fertilior seges est alienis semper in agris
> Vicinumque pecus grandius huber habet.

> [The harvest is more luxuriant in the fields of others,
> And the neighbor's cows have larger udders.]

## 12

### *How Gonnella proved to Marquis Nicolò*
### *that in Ferrara there was a*
### *multitude of doctors*

℞ GONNELLA, an amusing and modest jester in his
day, was asked once by the Marquis Nicolò of Ferrara
what guild or profession had the most representatives
in Ferrara. Without hesitating he replied, "Who
doesn't know that the doctors are the most numerous
here?"

Then the Marquis said, "It is evident that you are not well acquainted with the guilds and craftsmen of this city; for, counting the citizens and the foreigners, Ferrara has two or three physicians at the most."

To this Gonnella replied, "One can easily see that Your Excellency's mind is taken up with much more important matters, and that you therefore have no knowledge of your city or its citizens."

"Suppose I show you that what you say is false," added the Marquis.

"Suppose I show Your Excellency that it is true," said Gonnella.

So there was set up between them a penalty or a bet to be paid by the one who was found to have lied.

Early the following morning, Gonnella placed himself by the door of the cathedral, with his face and his throat all bundled up with a fur. To all those who, going into the church, asked him what was the matter with him, he answered that he had a toothache; whereupon, everyone of them told him some remedy against the pain. He took down the name of each one and the prescription he had been given. Thus, going through the city in search of toothache remedies, after having asked all those he had met, he ended up with a list of more than three hundred people who had suggested to him what medicine to use against toothache.

One morning, when he had done this, he went to the palace at the hour when he knew the Marquis was accustomed to having lunch. He arrived with his face and throat all bandaged up and pretended to be in great pain. Completely unsuspecting of Gonnella's trick, the Marquis said at once: "Gonnella, you must use the remedy that I am going to give you, and you will be grateful to me because you will be cured at once."

After Gonnella had jotted down the prescription,

he returned home and made an exact list of all the remedies he had been given, and of the names of the people who had given them to him; at the head of the list he wrote the name of the Marquis, and below, all the others in the order of their rank.

Three days later, pretending to be completely cured, he called on the Marquis and showed him the prescriptions he had been given for toothache; further, he asked him to pay the bet, saying that if he refused to pay it, he would bring him to trial, and with these words he showed him the list.

When the Marquis saw that he was at the head of the list of doctors, and that he was followed by so many other gentlemen, he was unable to keep from laughing; and confessing that he had lost the bet, he ordered that Gonnella be paid.

## 13

### Gonnella cuts off the upper lip of Marquis Nicolò's donkeys

THE Marquis Nicolò of Ferrara had had the tail of Gonnella's horse cut off secretly with a razor in the stable. When Gonnella saw that, he cut off the upper lip of certain donkeys that were kept in the same stable. When this was brought to the Duke's attention, he made no apologies: he simply asked that the damage be estimated; and in order to do this more accurately, he had the donkeys brought before him.

First they led in by the halter Gonnella's horse, which was wagging a stub of a tail; then the donkeys were led in one by one. When all the animals were brought before the Marquis and everybody saw and examined the horse's tail, the Marquis and all the others who were there broke into uncontrollable laughter. Then Gonnella said, "Neither you, Your Excellency, nor any-

one else here, serious and dignified though these gentlemen be, were able to refrain from laughing at this
spectacle. How do you expect these donkeys, simple
animals as they are, not to laugh when they see my
horse, whom they know so well, without a tail?" Whereupon there was another outburst of laughter, and Gonnella was absolved and praised as the prince of all
witty individuals and as a most charming master of
amusing pleasantries.

## 14
### Gonnella is duped by a peasant girl

SHORTLY afterwards, the same Gonnella ran into
a young woman who was tending goats. In order to make
sport of her, he said, "Beautiful girl, here is a silver
piece for you if you show me your parsley."

The young peasant girl accepted the condition and
the silver piece; and immediately, having seized an old
she-goat, she lifted its tail and said, "Here you are;
see, take a good look at the parsley you are asking
about."

## 15
### The King of Tunis has a pile of bones
### tossed at the feet of Queraldo during dinner

AMONG the senators of King Peter of Aragon there
was one called Queraldo, who had a very ugly face and
body but who was on the other hand a wise and capable
man. Once he had gone as an ambassador to the King
of Tunis, and he was invited to supper. Whereas the
Moors have the custom of eating seated on rugs that
cover the floors, the King had a table set up on trestles
for him, as we do in our country. Now, the King, who
was himself a witty person and delighted in practical

jokes, had all the bones collected secretly and tossed
at the feet of Queraldo, in such a way that he did not
notice anything. When supper was over and the tables
were cleared by order of the master of ceremonies, a
man who had been instructed by the King said, "What
are all those bones? It must certainly have been a wolf,
not a man, that ate here!"

Whereupon, Queraldo turned to the King and said,
"Apparently I have eaten with wolves, which eat the
meat and the bones, as these guests of yours have done;
whereas I, who am a man and a discreet person, have
eaten the meat and tossed away the bones on the floor
to feed and regale the dogs."

## 16

*Queraldo spits on the face*
*of the King's servant*

THE same Queraldo was taken by the King into a
room where everything was covered with gold and silk

materials, so that there was no place where one could spit without being censured for it. At that point, one of the King's servants, who had a very ugly face, came near him; and Queraldo—who wanted to amuse the King—immediately spat on the servant's face. The servant screamed and turned to the King [complaining of the insult he had been done]. Upon hearing the charge, Queraldo said, "Your Majesty, being filled with wonder by the splendor and pomp of this decor, in order not to soil any part of it—since I could not see a single dirty place in this room, except his ugly face—I spat on him, for I believed you kept him around for that very purpose."

## 17

### *Mariotta teaches a lesson*
### *to her lecherous husband*

MONA MARIOTTA, the wife of the Florentine merchant Antonio, was an amiable and charming lady. Having heard that her husband went out every night through the city, going after all the dishonest women he could find, Mariotta waited one night for him to return. When he returned, she, who was standing at the top of the stairs with a lighted torch, lifted up the front part of her gown and showed him what she had.

Upon seeing this, the husband shouted, "Goodness, Mariotta! Why the torch, and why are you naked?"

And she replied, "I wanted to show you that there is so much of this at home that it should be enough for you, so that you will stop tiring yourself out looking for more in the back alleys."

# VII

## *Leonardo da Vinci*

### *1452-1519*

# LEONARDO

LEONARDO was born out of wedlock to Ser Pietro d'Antonio, a notary public, in the little town of Vinci, in Tuscany. Around 1470, he started as an apprentice in the studio of Andrea del Verrocchio; and, along with painting, he began to study music, mathematics, and the natural sciences. In 1483, after his master and fellow apprentices had left Florence for other parts of Italy, Leonardo went to the court of Lodovico il Moro, in Milan, where he remained until 1499. At Lodovico's court, Leonardo attended not only to painting and sculpturing, but also to inventing and building war machines and to carrying out engineering projects for his patron. Further, he acted also as a sort of impresario for court festivals. After brief sojourns in Venice and in the service of Caesar Borgia, he returned to Florence where, among other activities, he painted the cartoons of the Battle of Anghiari. At that time he shuttled back and forth between Florence and Milan, devoting more and more time to natural science and to anatomy. In 1513 he went to Rome, where he was under the patronage of Giuliano de' Medici, brother of Pope Leo X. At one point, Leo X forbade him to pursue his anatomical studies any further. In Bologna, where he had gone for a meeting between Pope Leo X and King Francis I of France, he met the latter, who invited him to accompany him to France. Leonardo accepted the invitation; and in 1516, he went to France and took up his abode in the castle of Cloux, near Amboise, where he died in 1519.

Leonardo was essentially a great artist and a most

gifted scientist. He liked to call himself "omo sanza lettere," a man without letters; but his numerous treatises do not bear that out.

Like many other writers who were not actually bent on making a real collection of anecdotes, Leonardo liked to intersperse facetious stories in his writings; and he recorded about twenty of them. Not all the anecdotes of Leonardo are original, but they are couched in a clear, concise, and lively style. Most of them are salacious, as was the fashion of the time.

## *Two friars, a merchant and a chicken*

AT certain times of the year, Gray Friars observe certain fasting rules of theirs and do not eat meat in their monasteries; however, when they are traveling, since they live on charity, they have permission to eat what is placed before them. Now, it happened that during one of these trips, two Gray Friars arrived at an inn at the same time as a petty merchant and sat down at the same table. Since it was a simple little inn, only a single boiled chicken was brought onto the table; whereupon, seeing that this would be hardly enough for himself, the merchant turned to the Friars and said: "If I recall correctly, at this time of the year you are not allowed to eat any type of meat in your monasteries." Upon hearing this, the Friars were compelled to say by their rule that it was true, with no quibbling over it. The petty merchant's wish was fulfilled, and thus he ate the whole chicken; and the Friars managed as best they could.

After lunch, such as it was, the three table-companions parted company; but when they had gone a distance, they came across a large river of a certain depth. The Friars because they were poor, and the merchant because he was miserly, decided to ford the river; and, out of good fellowship, one of the Friars —who was barefoot—accepted to carry the merchant on his back.

It happened that, when the Friar was in the middle of the river, he also remembered his rule; so, like St. Christopher, he stopped, turned his head toward the man who was weighing him down, and said: "Tell me, do you have any money on you?"

He replied: "You know very well that I do; how

could a merchant like me travel around otherwise?"

"Alas," said the Friar, "our rule forbids us to carry any money on us," and he threw him immediately into the water.

Whereupon, the merchant realized that the Friar had wittily avenged himself of his trick; blushing with shame, he smiled and accepted the retaliation philosophically.

## 2

### *The painter's blessing*

ON a Holy Saturday, as is customary, a priest was making the rounds of his parish, blessing homes with holy water. He came into the room of a painter, and as he sprinkled holy water over one of his paintings, the painter turned to him angrily and asked him why he was wetting his paintings. Then the priest said that it was the custom, and that it was his duty to carry it out. He added that he was doing the right thing, for he who does good can expect the same or better in return; it is God's promise that for every good thing one does on earth, one will receive a hundredfold from above.

The painter waited for the priest to leave his house, and then he went to the window and threw a large bucketful of water on top of him, saying: "Here is the hundredfold that is coming to you from above, as you said you would get for the good you were doing me with your holy water, which ruined half of my paintings."

### 3
### *Pythagoras is right*

℘ A CERTAIN man wished to prove with the authority of Pythagoras that he had been in this world other times, but another man interrupted him and did not give him a chance to finish his argumentation. Then the first man said to him, "And to prove to you that I was in this world previously, I recall that you were a miller." Whereupon, stung by these words, the second man agreed that what he had said was true; for by the same token, he recalled that the other had been the ass that used to carry his flour.

### 4
### *The provident friend*

℘ A MAN stopped associating with a friend of his because the latter often spoke evil of his friends. One day the deserted friend complained bitterly with his crony and finally begged him to tell him the reason that had made him forget their close friendship. Whereupon, he replied, "I do not wish to associate with you any longer because I like you; and I do not want it to happen that when you speak evil of me with others, they will get a bad impression of you the way I did; therefore, if we no longer associate with each other, people will think that we are enemies; and when you— as you are wont to do—speak evil of me, you will not be blamed as much as if we associated with each other."

## 5
### *Consolation of a dying man*

A SICK man was at the point of death when he heard a knock at his door. He asked one of his servants who it was that was knocking, and he was told that it was a woman called Bona ["Good"]. Then the sick man raised his arms and thanked God in a loud voice. He then told his servant to let her in at once, so that he could see one good woman before he died; for in his whole life he had never seen one.

## 6
### *A poor reason*

A MAN was told to rise from his bed because the sun had already risen, and he replied, "If I had as long a journey to take and as many things to do as the sun, I would have risen too; but since the distance I have to cover is so short, I do not want to rise yet."

## 7
### *Points of view*

ONE man said to another, "Your eyes have taken on a strange color."

The other man replied, "That's because they are looking at your strange face."

## 8
### Knavish fire

℧ A WOMAN was washing clothes, and her feet were very red with cold. A priest who was passing by asked her with amazement whence that redness came, and the woman replied at once that it was the result of the fire she had burning below. Then the priest seized that part of him that was responsible for his being a priest instead of a nun, and drawing close to her, with a sweet and soft voice begged her to be so kind as to light that candle for him.

## 9
### A proof of affection

℧ TWO fellows were walking at night along a dark, unfamiliar street. The one who was walking ahead broke air noisily; whereupon, his companion said, "Now I know that you love me."

"How is that?" asked the other.

The first fellow replied, "You offer me a belt [the Italian word *coreggia* means both "a belt" and "a fart"] so that I will not fall, and will not lose you."

## 10
### His ugliness was proof enough

℧ A MAN was saying that the strangest things were born in his native town. The man who had been listening to him acknowledged: "You were born there, and the odd shape of your person certainly bears out that what you say is the truth."

# VIII

## Ludovico Domenichi

### 1515-1564

# DOMENICHI

LUDOVICO DOMENICHI was born in Piacenza. He studied law at the universities of Pavia and Padua, and for a time he practiced law in his native city. He soon gave up the legal career, however, and devoted himself to literary pursuits. Upon the accusation of Anton Francesco Doni, formerly a close friend of his, he was tried by the tribunal of the Inquisition and cast into jail; but he was freed through the intercession of the Duchess Renata of Ferrara. He lived, at different times, in Venice, in Florence, and at the court of Urbino. He died in Florence.

Domenichi was a proof-reader, a historian, and a professional writer. He wrote extensively: we know of fifty-nine of his works. As we said in the Introduction, he prepared the largest collection of anecdotes in the Italian Renaissance.

In the preface to the first edition of his *Facetie et motti*,[1] Domenichi says that a Giovanni Mazzuoli, called Stradino, had lent him a "Bel libretto" ("a beautiful little book") of charming pleasantries and witticisms. He liked those stories so much that he reproduced—probably with some stylistic changes—most, if not all, of them, and then added a group of "Facetie raccolte per M. Ludovico Domenichi," [2] some of which, in reality, he had translated from the *Sermones conviviales* of Johannes Gast.

It has been proved by Albert Wesselski and confirmed by further studies of Gianfranco Folena that the four hundred-odd anecdotes of the first part of Domenichi's collection were almost certainly the work of Angelo Poliziano.

This first collection of Domenichi did not meet with much public favor, and it was reprinted only once with the consent of the author, in 1550.

After several years, however, Domenichi published in 1562 a second collection of anecdotes divided into six books; and in 1564, he published in Florence a third edition that contained seven books: *Facetie, motti et burle di diversi signori et persone private* ("Pleasantries, Witticisms and Jests of Several Gentlemen and Private Persons"). Shortly after, the author died.

This third edition of Domenichi's facetiae is quite different from the first, although it still retains nearly two hundred of the best to be found in the first edition, of which many can still be traced to the "Bel libretto."

For his last edition, Domenichi availed himself of numerous sources—Italian and also foreign. He tried to avoid those anecdotes that might have gotten him in trouble with religious authorities and powerful families, and attributed some of the "good" ones to actual or potential benefactors. Thus, the historical value of many of Domenichi's facetiae was lost; but the readers did not care, and his collection became one of the most read and pillaged—both because it was written rather elegantly and because, in its vastness and variety, it presented a good cross section of human comedy.

## *The old woman's prayer*

℘ A CERTAIN Duke of Milan was so hated for his unbearable cruelty that everybody prayed day and night for something bad to happen to him. Someone noticed that every day at sunrise a decrepit old woman entered a church and prayed God that he give the Duke health and a long life. The Duke, hearing about this and knowing very well that he did not deserve that for his virtues, sent for the old woman and asked her why she prayed to God for him every day. "I admit," she said, "that I have done this until now for a good reason. This is because when I was a young girl the Milanese had a very cruel lord, and I wished that he should fall from power and die. After he died he was succeeded by another who was no better than he, wherefore I believed once more that it would be to our great advantage if he were killed. Now you are our third lord, and you are more wicked and cruel than the first two. I fear, therefore, that after your death you will be succeeded by someone worse than you are; and so I never stop praying God to let you live for a long time." The tyrant was too ashamed to put to death that little woman, who was so witty and so bold.

## 2

## *The dead husband*

℘ A MAN came before the gates of heaven; upon hearing St. Peter say to him, "Come and thou shalt sit by your wife," he replied at once, "By God, that I shall not do; if my wife is inside, I shall never go in. For, if while I was alive I never had one moment's peace or rest with her, now that I am dead and have a lot of free time, how could I be with her all the time and be in peace?"

## 3

### *The nun who did not scream*

❦ WHEN I was a boy, I once heard a sermon delivered by a Dominican monk who had been born with the gift of oratory! In order to awaken the faithful who were asleep before him, he told this tale: Once a nun had sinned with a man and was with child. When the abbess became aware of this, she called her before the chapter of nuns and reprimanded her for having brought such shame on the convent.

The nun tried to exculpate herself by saying that she had been done violence to, saying, "There came into my room a young man who was much stronger than I, and I would have resisted him in vain. I was attacked, so do not accuse me of having sinned."

Then the abbess said, "You would not have sinned if you had screamed as our rule tells us to do."

Whereupon the nun replied, "Of course I would have screamed, but we were in the dormitory, where our rule is to serve in silence!"

## 4

### *Two portraits by Raphael*

❦ POPE JULIUS [3] had the rooms in which he lived painted by Raphael, a very excellent painter. In one of the rooms he had himself painted kneeling during Mass, and on the opposite wall, as he was returning

from Belvedere carried by his footmen. In the latter
portrait the colors were much more intense than in the
former, and some people blamed Raphael and said that
he had made a mistake not to use the same colors in
both portraits. Marco Antonio Colonna [4] intervened
and told the faultfinders that they were wrong and that
Raphael had indeed observed decorum; for, whereas
the Pope was sober during Mass, upon returning from
Belvedere, his face was flushed and ruddy because he
had indulged in drinking.

## 5

### The adulterous wife

A PEASANT had a dishonest and shameful wife, who
had been adulterous on various occasions. Feeling quite
disturbed by the whole thing, he complained about her
to his father-in-law and threatened to send her back to
him. The father-in-law tried to console his son-in-law
and said to him, "Pluck up courage, son, and let her
go on with her ways for a while; for some day she will
reform just like her mother did. When her mother, who
is my wife, was young, she too, as is customary, had her
escapades; but now that she is old, she is the best
woman in town. I am sure her daughter will follow in
her footsteps."

## 6

### Woman overboard!

DURING a raging storm at sea, all the passengers of
a ship were ordered to throw their heaviest possessions
overboard. The first thing that one of them threw over-

board was his wife, saying that he had nothing heavier or anything that weighed more heavily on him than she.

## 7

### *A thief should know better*

℞ COCCHINO, who was very poor, lived in a little house with no furniture or anything in it; so he never locked the door. One night a thief entered the house, went into Cocchino's bedroom and searched all over to see if he could find something to steal. When Cocchino heard him, he let him rummage about for a while; then he said, "Go on rummaging to your heart's content; I am anxious to see if you can find here at night what I cannot find in the daytime."

## 8

### *"There was a rickety old mill"*

℞ THIS proverbial phrase is thrown in the face of one who tells a lie and cannot defend it. A man called Regola was saying that he had been in a shipwreck and that he had swum to, and found shelter in, a deserted place where there was nothing to eat. Being asked, "How did you survive?" he replied that he had eaten a German whom he had broiled on hot embers. And being asked again, "Where did you get the fire?" he said that he always brought along a piece of steel for a gunflint. And being pressed further with, "Where did you get the wood?" he quickly added, "There was a rickety old mill near there, and drop dead!"

## 9
### *Four young brides*

℘ ONE day a beautiful young woman was with a group of women who were talking about husbands.

One of the women said, "When I got married, I hid myself!"

Another said, "I refused to take off my shirt."

Another, "I wouldn't let him touch me."

When the beautiful girl who had remained silent was asked, she said, "I wish my husband had done all I would have let him do!"

## 10
### *A pair of large trousers*

℘ AMONG the house-servants of Pietro Marzi was a young and showy German servant who, in keeping with the dishonest custom of the time, used to wear some

unbecoming long trousers that reached down to his
ankles—a truly barbarian and uncivilized fashion that
was stupidly tolerated by tradition. As this young man
carried out his house chores minding his own business,
every time the wife, the daughter, and the daughter-in-
law of Pietro saw him, they looked at him with amazement and smiled mischievously on account of those huge
and fierce trousers. Pietro noticed this on several occasions. And since he was very witty and even licentious
when he spoke and always spoke his mind when something came to him on the spur of the moment, regardless of whether it was in the presence of women, he
called the German before him one day and asked him,
"Arrigo, what have you got in those trousers?"

"Nothing, master," Arrigo replied.

However Pietro insisted on seeing what he had in
his trousers; and after Arrigo had pulled out a handker-
chief, a ball, and a wallet, Pietro turned to the women,
who were perhaps expecting to see something else,
and said to them, "Now, women, you see that he does
not have in his trousers all you had thought"; and he
left them there filled with shame and embarrassment.

## 11

### *The daughter who did not want to get married*

THERE was a father who had three marriageable
daughters; and since the young men of the town kept
asking him for the hand of one of them—whichever he
wanted to marry off first—he replied that he wanted
first to find out how his daughters felt about getting
married. Upon learning that no one of them wanted
a husband, he said, "Let us draw lots and let chance
decide."

Thus, he had a basin full of water brought in and asked his daughters to dip their hands in the basin and draw them out all together. Then he told them that it was his wish that the one whose hands would dry first should be the first one to get married. While they reiterated that they did not want to get married, the youngest, pretending that she did not want a husband, kept shaking her hands saying, "I do not want a husband: I do not want a husband!" Thus, on account of that violent shaking, her hands were the first to dry.

## 12
### The girl with the long nose

AS A young man was kissing a girl with a long nose, he said, in order to appear facetious and witty in his speech, "My dear girl, I am offering you my lips to kiss you in vain, for your nose prevents them from reaching your mouth."

The young woman blushed violently with anger; and feeling that she had been rudely stung, she said, "Since my nose prevents your mouth from getting close to mine, why don't you kiss me where I haven't got a nose!"

## 13
### The Roman thieves

SOME expert and bold Roman burglars, who had watched for several days a rich merchant's store that was located on Banchi Street, decided to rob him one night. After they had broken into the store with their special tools, they began to remove everything it contained. It so happened that, while they were busy load-

ing and carrying away the merchandise, the Chief of
Police passed by with his men; and seeing that there
were people going in and out of the store in the middle
of the night, he stopped filled with amazement and
asked what was going on. Whereupon, one of the
burglars came to the door with a broom in his hand,
pretending to be sweeping, and he said, "Captain, the
owner of this store has just died; and for certain reasons we are clearing out his things."

The Chief of Police remarked, "It's funny, but I
don't hear anybody weeping inside."

And the shrewd thief replied, "They certainly will
weep tomorrow morning!"

## 14

### A poor selection

AFTER a long and painful debate over the election
of a prince, the choice fell on one whom, out of respect,
I shall not mention. This had come about because of
the numerous disagreements among the electors, who
ended up by choosing an individual who was quite unworthy of that principality. When Umore [5] from
Bologna was asked what he thought of that election,
he, without stopping to think a single moment, replied
that those electors had imitated the fly, which circles
hither and thither for a long time and finally settles on
a heap of manure.

## 15

### The courtier who greeted an old prostitute

IN ROME a cardinal was looking through the blinds
of the window and saw one of his courtiers doffing his

hat before Angela del Moro, the "mother superior"
of the courtesans of that city. This shocked the Cardinal no end for he felt that the gentleman, who had the
reputation of being a most dignified person, had neg-
lected the dignity of his station. Wherefore, at lunch
time, when all his courtiers were present, in order to
reprimand the gentleman for what he had done and at
the same time in order to taunt a Brother who was
taken with Angela, he said, "Who was that lady whom
you greeted and honored by removing your hat this
morning in front of our house?"

The gentleman, who was very open-minded, replied
without hesitation: "The lady whom I honored was
Angela del Moro."

Whereupon the Cardinal added, "Is your sense of
decorum so low that you so openly honor a public
prostitute?"

Upon which the good gentleman, noticing that all
the courtiers had turned in his direction and that while
waiting for an answer they were deriding him, not
knowing then and there what else to do, he said, tinged
with a noble blush, "My Lord, one of the first precepts
my tutor taught me when I was a young boy was this
one: *Semper veneranda senectus* ["Old age must always be honored"]."

Moved to laughter by this witty reply, the Cardinal
turned to his Brother and said, "Now it is up to you to
heal the wound that he, defending himself so cleverly,
has inflicted upon you." And it was the Cardinal's intention to reproach him his unbecoming love for an old
whore.

## 16
### *The stolen capon*

❧ AS A young boy, while he still lived with his father,
Marco Cadamosto stole from him a lovely fat capon
in order to enjoy it with his friends at the tavern.
When his father, who had planned for a long time to
eat the capon during the coming carnival, heard about
it, he flew into a rage against his son: he drove him
out of the house and repeated many times that he didn't
want him ever to return home. As from day to day his
anger did not subside, some of his relatives censured
him severely for having driven his own son out of
doors on such a small account. Whereupon, turning to
them full of indignation, he answered: "Our glorious
God, who is all perfect, drove Adam, our first father,
out of the Garden of Eden for having eaten an apple,
which put all mankind in jeopardy. God did this to the
one he had created with his own hands, of his own free
will, and with such superb art. And now you are stunned
because I have driven out of my house one whom I
created in the dark, accidentally, and without hard
work, because he has eaten against my specific command such a handsome fat capon, with which I had
planned to celebrate the carnival festivities?"

## 17
### *The hair was white, but the beard was black*

❧ WHEN POPE PAUL III was in Ancona and heard
that in that city there was also Marretto, a broker
from Siena, who was an intelligent and wise man, con-

sidered to be one of the shrewdest and craftiest men of his day, he sent for him, since he was a prince who enjoyed the company of clever men.

After they had talked for a while, the Pope asked him how old he was. Marretto replied that he was sixty-one; and since he noticed that His Holiness didn't quite believe him, he took off his cap, uncovering a head of perfectly white hair. The Pope was stunned and said that, judging by his beard, which was not yet gray, he didn't look over forty.

"Don't let that surprise you, Holy Father," rejoined Marretto, "for my hair is twenty years older than my beard."

## 18

### *Michelangelo's revenge*

IN OUR TIME, Pope Paul III has been a prince of the rarest prudence and most marvelous cleverness. Once, it happened that messer Biagio,[6] who was his master of ceremonies, went before him to complain of the insult he thought Michelangelo Buonarroti had done him by painting him in the chapel of the Last Judgment in Rome, beset and tormented by the devils of hell. This, Michelangelo had done because he had felt hurt that messer Biagio, in his presumptuousness, had insisted on seeing his marvelous painting before the proper time. Realizing that his attempts at consoling him were all futile and that Biagio kept insisting that he protest to Michelangelo, in order to get rid of him the Pope said: "Messer Biagio, you know that God has given me power over heaven and earth; but since my authority does not extend over hell, you will have to be patient if I cannot get you out of there."

## 19
### *Machiavelli's improvisation*

꙳ NOT long ago there was in Florence a fine club made up of gifted and skillful men who, after their customary literary discussions and other intellectual pursuits, sometimes practiced improvising verses accompanying themselves on the lyre. They did this in the presence of beautiful ladies of that city, perhaps with the hope that their beauty would inspire some lovely poetic concepts. In order to prevent any previous preparation, they would open a volume of ancient poetry, such as Ovid's *Metamorphoses,* and they would improvise a tune on the topic they had chanced upon. One day one of the gentlemen wanted to hear Nicolò Machiavelli improvise, and he chanced to open the book where the fable of Venus and Mars was narrated. After Machiavelli had briefly described in his first few lines how Vulcan, having become aware of his wife's adultery and wishing to avenge himself, had built the very fine iron net with which to catch both lovers while they were making love, he concluded as follows:

> He flung out the net and with one cast caught
> Venus all naked. . . .

At that point he stopped, although he continued to strum the lyre as if he were searching for the missing words with which to complete the verse, when one of the ladies, who knew him better than the others, told him, "Hurry up and finish, messer Nicolò; for if you think about it too long, it will no longer count as an improvisation."

Wherefore, with no further hesitation, Nicolò started from the beginning and said:

He flung out his net and caught in one cast
Venus all naked, and Mars . . . quite erect.

"Oh, goodness!" said those ladies, who were blushing with shame. "What did you ever say, messer Nicolò!"

Whereupon, he replied, "That lady rushed me so that I did not stop to consider what I was saying!"

## 20
## *Married eggs*

℣ A GOOD and very intimate friend of Bartolomeo Amannati went to have lunch at his house on a Friday. While lunch was being prepared, he, as he was wont to do, wandered into the kitchen, where he found the maid who was preparing what we call "married eggs." And since the poor woman had given her daughter in marriage to a good-for-nothing, he tried to tease her by saying, "Mona Fabiana" (for this was her name), "you are better at marrying eggs than your daughters!"

Whereupon, turning to him angrily, she replied, "You could say that if I had given my daughter to you!"

## 21
## *Raphael's reply to a lady*

℣ RAPHAEL from Urbino, a remarkable and most excellent painter, was painting the loggia in Agostino Chigi's garden in Rome. He had painted many Goddesses and Graces there, and also a very large Polyphemus and a thirteen-year-old Mercury. One morning there came to the loggia a lady who considered herself cultured and intelligent; she admired and praised the paintings highly, and then said: "Undoubtedly all these figures are most excellent; but for the sake of modesty I wish you would paint a lovely rose or a vine-leaf on Mercury's shame."

Raphael said smiling: "Pardon me, madam, it was very inconsiderate of me." And then he added: "But why didn't you ask me to do the same for Polyphemus, whom you praised so much a while ago, and who has a much larger shame?"

## 22

### *A real antique!*

MESSER FRANCESCO BERNI,[7] formerly a canon in the cathedral of Santa Liberata, is well known for his wit and his jests. One day in Florence he was in the company of a secretary of the Cardinal of San Giorgio, who was very fond of antiques. When the secretary asked him whether he knew of any antiques that he might like to see, Francesco Berni replied that he possessed a very fine and most ancient antique, and that he would be happy to show it to him provided he did not count on acquiring it and was willing to promise not to tell anyone about it, for it cost him a great deal of money and he was not about to sell it. The secretary gave his word, and messer Francesco took him to his house for lunch. After lunch he took him to a bedroom where he showed him his ninety-four-year-old grandmother. And he said: "Don't you think that this is a fine antique?"

## 23
### The defective sonnet

℘ MESSER MARCO DA LODI had given one of his sonnets to Pope Clement to read as a pastime. As the Pope was reading it, he said, when he came to the second or third line: "Look, messer Marco; this verse is one syllable short."

Immediately messer Marco replied: "Don't let that bother you, Holy Father; for in reading the rest of the poem you will certainly find a line with one syllable too many, and that will make up for the short one."

## 24
### The age of a man and of a donkey

℘ TWO CASTILIAN gentlemen, Don Francisco de Anaia, who was old and very wise, and Don Diego de Agro, who was young but senseless and uncouth, wrote a love letter to the same lady at the same time. Later, in order to embarrass his rival, the young swain asked him in the presence of the lady how old he was. The old wooer replied: "I don't really know exactly, but I know very well that an ass of twenty years is older than a man of seventy."

## 25
### Reply of a prostitute to a lady

℘ THE paving of a certain street in Rome was done from the tax paid by prostitutes. One day Giulia from Ferrara bumped against a lady on that street, and the latter began insulting her angrily. Giulia replied: "Pardon me, madam, for I know that on this street you have more right than I do!"

## 26

### *A matter of precedence*

A CERTAIN gentleman was about to make a parley before Gismondo, Duke of Austria, when, unable to restrain himself, he broke air loudly. Whereupon, turning to his behind he said so that everyone heard him: "If you want to speak, it won't be necessary that I speak." And, thus, with great aplomb he continued his speech. This so pleased the Duke, who was very fond of witticisms, that he treated him with great honor.

## 27

### *The young husband who boasted*
### *of having seduced a young woman*

A CERTAIN young man from Parma, who had been married only a few days, was at a window with his bride when he saw a beautiful young woman going to Mass. He turned to his bride and said: "I want to make you laugh. See that young woman who is passing below our window? Well, before she got married, I was intimate with her several times; but she was so harebrained that she went and told her mother everything, and we narrowly missed a big scandal."

Then, his wife replied: "What a fool, what a scatterbrain she is! I was intimate over a hundred times with the cart driver, with the manservant, and with our sharecropper, and I never told my mother a word about it."

## 28
### The wife's confession

A CERTAIN peasant, wishing to hear his wife's confession, hid himself behind the place where the priest sat. Among other sins, the woman confessed that she had betrayed her husband. The priest, at the end of her confession, wanted to absolve her and began first with the sin of adultery. At that point the peasant jumped out of his hiding-place and said: "Go right ahead and absolve her of the other sins; as for this sin, I will punish her in such a way that you won't have to give her any other penance."

## 29
### The shipwrecked Sicilian

A SICILIAN was shipwrecked and lost a whole load of dried figs. As often happens, he was washed ashore. He sat on the beach to dry himself; and, seeing that the sea had become calm as if to invite him to sail again, he said: "You damned sea! I know very well what you want: you want some more dry figs!"

## 30
### Of a man about to be hanged

AS BARDELLA from Mantua was being taken to the gallows, someone who was trying to comfort him said to him: "Be of good cheer; this evening you will dine with the Virgin Mary and with the Apostles."

Bardella replied, "Please, you go in my place; for today I am fasting."

## 31
### The blind man and the virgin

A MAN blind in one eye had taken as a wife a young girl whom he believed to be a virgin; but she proved otherwise, and he was reproving her harshly. And she replied, "Why should you want to have me whole, when you yourself are blind and have only one eye?"

Then the husband said, "My enemies are responsible for my loss."

And the girl said to him, "And my friends for mine."

## 32
### The jester and the little fish

AS A jester was sitting at the table with certain gentlemen, he was served some very tiny fish, and they, large ones. Wherefore, the jester began picking up a handful of those small fish, and putting them first close to his mouth and then to his ear, pretending to be talking secretly to them; and at last he began to weep. Whereupon those gentlemen asked him why he was crying, and he said, "My father was a fisherman, and he had the misfortune of drowning in a river. I asked these little fish if they ever ran into my father anywhere, but they replied that they are too young to know such a thing and that I should ask those bigger fish who are older."

Upon hearing that, the gentlemen had some bigger fish given to him in order that he might ask them—or rather, devour them.

## 33
### The husband's revenge

℃ THERE was a simple man who loved his wife so much that he said he would never survive seeing her touched by another man. Not long afterwards, while he and his wife were walking through the woods, they met a knight who seized the woman for his pleasure and left his horse and his clothes in the husband's care. When the woman and the knight returned, she scolded her husband for letting her fall into the hands of another man. "Hush!" he said. "I didn't stand here idle, I tore his cloak in several places."

## 34
### King Alfonso of Naples and his courtiers

℃ ONCE, King Alfonso of Naples was at sea on his flagship. Some of his favorite courtiers who were with him went on the stern to pay their respect to the King, as it was their custom, and found him watching some sea birds that were flying around the galley; when some scraps fell from the galley, they flew in that direction. And those that caught them immediately flew away. After the King had watched those birds for a while, he suddenly turned to his gentlemen and said, "Some of my favorite courtiers remind me of those birds—because after they have fought over an appointment or a favor from me, as soon as they receive it, they go elsewhere."

## 35

### *As warm as an oven*

℧ IN ORDER to buy himself a velvet coat, a doctor of laws from Brescia had sold an oven. One day, although it was rather warm, he was wearing his coat in the company of many gentlemen; and wiping his face often, he was complaining of the excessive heat. Whereupon, one of those gentlemen who knew the genealogy of his coat, said, "I am not at all surprised that you are so warm; after all, you are wrapped up in an oven."

## 36

### *He deserved to be burned*

℧ A BOLOGNESE gentleman who was known for his studies on the squaring of the circle went to call on a student of his, who was a most handsome and well-mannered young man. As it was winter, he found him seated by the fire. The student rose and received him cheerfully and courteously; then he turned to a servant and asked him to bring in more wood and to toss it into the fire. The gentleman said that it wasn't at all cold, and that there was no need of more wood; for the fire was plenty warm.

At which, the student said smiling, "What do you mean, sir? The fire could never be as warm as you deserve!"

## 37
### *Fidelity of mouth*

A YOUNG bride was so insistently solicited by a
suitor that she yielded her whole body to him with the
exception of her mouth. Although they slept in each
other's arms many times, she never granted him a single
kiss. When he finally asked her what was the reason
for it, she said, "When I got married, my mouth
promised fidelity and loyalty to my husband; and my
mouth will keep its promise. Therefore, give up any
hope of ever receiving a kiss from me. You can do what
you like with my body, but I'd rather die than break my
promise."

## 38
### *Circumcision or baptism?*

THERE was once in Venice a Jewess who was so
beautiful and charming that I myself tried to persuade

her to become a Christian, but she gave me a very good answer. In short, she wanted to tell me that circumcision was as good as baptism. Thus, she asked me how high we Christians held baptism, and I replied that we have the highest reverence for it and that without it the door of heaven remains shut. In contrast, she told me, Jewish women don't think very highly of circumcision; and when I asked her for the reason of this, she said that they wished that something were added to their men instead of subtracted.

## 39

### *He should have returned the first vase sooner*

COUNT LODOVICO of Canossa, who was Bishop of Baiussa, had in his house in Rome a beautiful set of silverware, which included many vases exquisitely decorated in various ways. Among other things, he had a pitcher whose lid was carved in the shape of a tiger, and a saltcellar shaped like a crab.

A gentleman, who shall remain nameless, was very fond of the mentioned pitcher; and one day, with the excuse that he wanted to have it copied for his own use, he sent his servant to borrow it. But instead of returning it, he kept it for over two months, thinking that Count Lodovico would forget it. However, he was asked to return it, and he did. Then he asked whether he might borrow the saltcellar, which, as we said above, was fashioned in the shape of a crab; he was determined to keep this one forever. The Bishop sensed that this might be the case and sent word to him that, if the tiger, which is a very swift animal, had taken two months to return home, the crab, which is the slowest of animals, at that rate would take years. And that for that reason he was unwilling to let the crab out of the house.

## 40
### *Life in jail is no life*

℘ A MAN named Bragiacca had spent thirty years at Le Stinche, a jail in Florence. When he was sixty years old, he was asked his age; and he said that he was thirty. "What's the matter with you?" asked a by-stander. "You spent thirty years at the Stinche!"

He replied, "Nobody could ever make me say that I lived during those thirty years!"

## 41
### *Not everything can be straightened out*

℘ AT THE beginning of the papacy of Leo X, Cardinal Gurgense was sent by Emperor Maximilian to settle— so people said—Italian affairs. He was received with the greatest honors; and as is customary in Florence and in other towns, all the trumpeteers and the other musicians of the city went to serenade him in order to receive a tip. There also went along a certain Pappino, who played the drum and was very facetious; but he was crippled, twisted, and had a hump on his back, so that he looked like a monster. After Pappino had ad-dressed several pleasantries to the Cardinal, in order to make him laugh he said, "I'd like a favor from Your Excellency: they say here in Florence that you came from Germany to straighten out all crooked things. I beg you to straighten me out also, for I need it as much as anyone else!"

## 42
### *He was not a very good doctor*

TO A doctor who called on him and asked him whether he had any ailments, messer Alfonso Cambi replied, "None, because I don't have you as my physician."

The doctor said, "Why do you reprove me if you have not tried me?"

Messer Alfonso answered, "If I had tried you I wouldn't be reproving you, for I would be dead."

## 43
### *A biting retort*

WHEN a short, homely young man saw certain pregnant women going to the church of St. Margaret, who is their protectress, he said to a group of his friends, "Those women are going to St. Margaret's in order to have beautiful children."

Whereupon, one of the women turned around and said to him, "It is evident that your mother did not go."

## 44
### *The generosity of Cardinal Ippolito de' Medici*

IN OUR time Cardinal Ippolito de' Medici was a most generous and virtuous prince. He had a retinue of several hundred people; and this required a considerable expense, which far exceeded his income—large and bounteous though it was.

At the time when Charles V was crowned Emperor
by Pope Clement VII in Bologna, the Cardinal was
with the Pope; and there he entertained all sorts of
people with great courtesy and splendor, as was in keeping with his magnanimity. One day the Cardinal had
gone horseback riding; and the Pope who, like the very
thrifty and miserly individual that he was, had often
found it necessary to rebuke the Cardinal, but with no
success, for his excessive lavishness, decided to discover
whether there was some way of controlling and curtail-
ing his nephew's prodigality. He sent for the Cardinal's
majordomo and asked him for the list of the people at
court who were on the Cardinal's payroll. When he saw
that incredibly long list, he was shocked by the large
number of names; he took a pen and began crossing out
all those that seemed unnecessary and useless to his
nephew's needs. Then, he returned the list to the majordomo and said to him, "You will tell my nephew in
my name that he must dismiss all the people I have
crossed out from his list and that he does not need so
many servants."

In the evening, upon the Cardinal's return to the
palace, the majordomo handed him the list and gave
him the Pope's message. Whereupon, the Cardinal
replied at once: "His Holiness is right when he says
that I do not need all the servants he has crossed out;
but since they need me, if you value at all my favor, do
not dismiss any of them."

<h1 style="text-align:center">45</h1>
Debate between a doctor and a painter

❧ ONCE a doctor poked fun at the work of an excellent painter saying that it was not worth very much.
The painter, who flew off the handle at the slightest

provocation, resented being scolded like a blockhead;
and instead of taking the whole thing in good spirits,
he wanted to get even with the doctor and began vex-
ing him: he launched headlong against the whole med-
ical profession, resorting to the common insults that
are spoken every day against physicians—namely that
without fear of punishment they kill people left and
right every day and that there is no denying the veracity
of the proverb that says that a young doctor fills a
whole cemetery with his mistakes. But the doctor re-
buffed that adage with a pleasantry. He said, "Well
spoken, master. In this respect your profession is much
luckier than ours, because the excellence and the blunders of a profession are judged in the light of day. But,
whereas it is true that masterpieces of art are seen and
judged in the daytime, just as the patients we have
cured can be seen about during the day, when it comes
to blunders, fortune has been much more favorable to
us; for she removes ours from before people's eyes
and hides them underground."

## 46
### Three quick replies of Dante Alighieri

❦ IN HIS day, the famous poet Dante Alighieri was
considered to be very quick-witted in giving impromptu
replies.

One day he was returning from a journey when three
Florentine men saw him from a distance. They recognized him; and, as they were riding about for pleasure,
they spurred their horses in Dante's direction. When
they got close to him, in order to test his gift for quick
replies, all three of them asked him a question—each
in rapid succession. The first one said to him, "Good
day, messer Dante." The second asked him, "Whence

are you coming?" And the third one asked, "Is the
river high?"

Without slowing down his horse, and without paus-
ing between replies, he answered as follows: "Good
morning; from the fair; up to your buttocks."

## 47
### *The young wife*

ℰ  A MAN who was well along in years married a very
young woman. They had been married a few months
when summer came; and since he was a well-to-do
gentleman who was accustomed to living in comfort,
he did not like to sleep with his wife during the hot
weather. So he had two beds made up—one for himself in the anteroom, and the other in the bedroom for
his wife. Then he said to his wife, "Love, it is customary with all the noblemen of this city to have two
beds set up during the summer: one for the wife, and
the other for the husband. This is done with the sole
purpose of avoiding the discomforts of heat. I believe
we should also follow this custom to avoid this nui-
sance." His wife did not agree with him at all, and she
turned up her nose at the whole idea. Whereupon her
husband added, "Now see here, darling; this does not
mean that we shall not be often together, because the
door between your room and mine will stay open all the
time; and when I want to play with you, I shall whistle
and you will come to me. And when we are through, you
will go back to your bed: in this manner, each one of
us will be most comfortable."

The wife agreed. During the following nights she
listened quietly for her husband's signal. One night,
after having waited in vain several nights, and thinking
that her husband was waiting too long, she took heart

and went into his room. She woke him up, and in her native tongue she said to him, "Messere, did you whistle?" And when he replied that he hadn't, she went on: "I thought you had whistled." Upon her husband's reiterated denials, she finally said to him, "If you didn't whistle, I did." And having lain down next to him, she forced him to pay the marriage debt.

## 48
### *The omelets were wafer-thin*

MESSER Marco from Lodi was known to all the courtiers in Rome, where he was in the service of a cardinal. One Friday he wandered into the kitchen just before lunchtime and found that the cooks were making many omelets, which the head cook was stacking one on top of the other in order to serve them later to the courtiers of that palace. For no apparent reason at all, Marco picked up a large rock that happened to be nearby and let it fall on top of the stack of omelets, ruining them all. A great clamor went up in the kitchen, and from there it spread throughout the entire house. Many rose against Marco, complaining bitterly of the dirty trick he had played, which was directed to all the luncheon guests. Messer Marco did his best to apologize, saying that he had not meant to cause any harm; all he had meant to do was to keep those extremely thin and light omelets from being picked up by a draft and blown away.

## 49
### *Messer Marco's mule*

THIS same messer Marco was at the breakfast table with the other courtiers one morning when there was placed before him a dish of very tough, black meat. He immediately jumped to his feet and dashed out of the breakfast room uttering woeful groans. When he returned shortly afterward smiling from ear to ear, the other table companions asked him why he had left grumbling, whereas now he seemed so cheerful and happy. He replied as follows: "Dear friends and brethren, I confess to you that when they brought me this meat, which you can all see, judging by its color, smell, taste, and toughness, I immediately came to the conclusion that it was the flesh of my mule. Filled with this suspicion, I ran to the stable to see whether that was actually the case. When I found my mule alive and kicking, I breathed a sigh of relief; and that is the reason for my cheerfulness."

## 50
### Epitaph for a boy

FRANCESCO FILELFO [8] was considered an excellent man of letters in his day; and for this reason people often asked him to deliver orations, write epitaphs, and other matters of the kind, to the point that he was completely irritated by these requests.

One day an irksome individual asked him with great insistence to write an epitaph for a young relative of his who had passed away. Francesco Filelfo refused several times in vain. Finally, overcome by the importunity of the man, he asked him the name of the deceased for whom he was to compose the epitaph; and he was told that his name was Giovanni Vitelli and that he had departed from this life at seventeen years of age. Messer Filelfo thought for a while; then he took a pen and wrote the following epitaph:

Iuppiter omnipotens Vituli miserere Joannis,
Quem mors praeueniens non sinit esse bouem.

(*Omnipotent Jupiter, have mercy on John Vituli* [the
Latin equivalent of Vitelli. The pun rests on the boy's
surname, which means also calf],
*Whom death prevented from growing into an ox.*)

## 51
### *Prostitution is not a contagious malady*

A CAPTAIN Concio became so taken with the many
beauties of a Roman courtesan named Vincenza Capista
that his excessive love for her led him to marry her
without the slightest consideration for his self-respect.
He took her to his home town, and there he held her
in great esteem and treated her as one treats a normal
wife. She went to parties and festivals, and she went
to church with the other women of the town, in ac-
cordance with the custom and practice of that province.

One day she went to church to hear Mass, and she
knelt to say her prayers next to one of the leading ladies
of that town. Vincenza noticed that as she was kneeling, the noblewoman rose to her feet, and, in order not
to remain next to her, was about to go to another pew
far from where she was—a clear proof that she did
not wish to associate with her. Vincenza then turned to
her and said in a loud voice: "Madam, do not leave this
place; for I assure you that my malady can be caught
only by those who desire it."

## 52
### *Compliment to a beautiful lady*

ONE summer day many gentlemen were gathered
for a party in the house of Countess Salamona, one of
the most beautiful and honorable ladies of the city.

Everyone was complaining of the extreme heat, and in
fact it was a very hot day. One of those gentlemen,
Signor Marc' Antonio Platone, said to the others, "Do
not be surprised, gentlemen, if the heat is so intense
here; for you are in the house of the Sun"—meaning,
in a poetic fashion, that because of her rare beauties,
that lady was like another sun.

### 53
### *How King Alfonso felt about neutrals*

WHEN King Alfonso [of Naples] heard that the
Sienese—who in the Italian war had remained neutral
between the opposing armies—at the end of the war
had been a prey to the soldiers of both armies, he said
that they had met with the same fate as those people
who live on the second floor of a three-story house, who
are plagued by the smoke of the people who live on the
first floor and by the urine of those who live on the
third.

### 54
### *The dead may be more alive than the living*

MESSER Lodovico Dolce,[9] a man of great intellect,
was reading some classical authors—something that he

did regularly. A friend of his went up to him and said,
"What are you doing here, hiding among the dead? It's
time that you came out with us who are alive."

"On the contrary," he replied; "they are still alive
because they are famous; whereas you are not alive
either in name or in deed, for you go on living like a
beast."

## 55
### Animals are wiser than men

SIGNOR GIORGIO GRADENIGO, a Venetian gentleman
of lofty ideals, used to say that among all the things
that filled him with amazement, this was the most as-
tonishing: animals, which do not have the use of reason, do not allow themselves to be ruled by a king who
is not superior to all others; whereas men, who call
themselves rational beings, often obey those princes
who are more stupid than four-footed animals.

## 56
### The Emperor stands above all others

DURING the Council of Constance, Emperor Gismondo [10] was rebuked by the Cardinal of Piacenza because he had used incorrect Latin in violation of gram-
matical rules. The Emperor promptly replied in a courteous tone: "If we stand above the law, why can't we
stand also above grammar?"

## 57
### Witty reply of Castruccio Castracane

CASTRUCCIO [11] had put to death a few members of
the Quartigiani family, who had plotted against him
in the city of Lucca. A friend of his who was having
supper with him said, "Lord, people are censuring you
severely because you treat your old friends so badly."

Whereupon he replied at once, "I am not dealing
with old friends, but rather with new enemies."

## 58
### A stinging reply

SIGNOR GIOVAN BATTISTA GIRALDI, who was a most
learned and talented man of letters, was approached
by a citizen of the city of Ferrara who wanted to walk
with him. The latter was not a bad fellow, but he was
uneducated. He said to him, "I do not want you to
walk alone."

Signor Giraldi replied, "I would be alone if I were
walking with you."

## 59
### He wanted wine, not water

A MISERLY gentleman dishonestly diluted the wine
of his servants with water. He was so niggardly that
if he had been able to do it, he would have extracted
their teeth to keep them from eating. One day he could
not refrain from saying to one of his servants who was

eating heartily, "When will that mill of a mouth of yours stop grinding?"

The young man replied, "It is not going to stop very soon because you are providing us with a lot of water!"

## 60

### *She could have been rich!*

IN THE countryside around Bevagna there was a peasant who had returned from Rome to spend carnival time at home. He was lying in bed with his wife, and she asked him how men managed with women in Rome. The husband told her that there were more than enough women in Rome.

"Do they get paid for it?" the wife asked.

"Of course," he replied.

"And how much does each one get?" she inquired.

"It depends," he answered. "People in our class pay sometimes a *grosso*,[12] sometimes a *carlino*." [12]

"Heavens!" she exclaimed, "if we had that custom here, Bebbetta's second son would surely owe me a lot of money!"

## 61

### *The shoes fitted better than the shoemaker thought*

THE CARDINAL of Monte was elected Pope, and was named Julius III. While the shoemaker was helping him put on the pontifical shoes, he, thinking that they were too tight for his feet, said: "Holy Father, they do not fit you."

"Go right ahead and put them on my feet," replied the Pope, "for no shoes ever fitted me better than these!"

## 62

### *A student plays a trick on a courtesan*

℘ A STUDENT from Pescia many times had solicited in fun a courtesan, pretending that he was in love with her and that he wanted to sleep with her; but she had never heeded him. One particular time he told her that he was very anxious to be with her and that if she let him sleep in her house, he would give her a gold *scudo*.[13] When the courtesan heard about the scudo, she yielded and said to him: "Since you say that you are in love with me, I want to please you; come this evening."

The student had a Lucchese *grosso* [14] gilded so that it looked like a real Lucchese scudo; then he had it pierced and he put it around his neck. When evening came, he went to the courtesan's house and found that she had set out some excellent marzipans, confections, and Greek wines for him and that she was expecting him to spend the night there.

The next morning he rose early because he said he had some matters to attend to; he took the counterfeit scudo from around his neck and said, "Madam, I should like you to do me a favor; for now I do not have much money: keep this scudo for me, which I wear around my neck out of devotion because it has touched all the holy relics in Rome; in a couple of days when I get my allowance, I will give you another scudo, and you can return this one to me. But, please, do not show this one to anyone; for many people have seen it on me, and they would recognize it and make fun of me." The good woman took it, put it away, and promised to save it for him.

After several days had gone by, and having seen that the young fellow was not coming back to exchange

the scudo he had left with her, she took it out; and looking at it more carefully in the daylight, she realized that
it was a gilt grosso. Filled with anger and disappoint-
ment, she went to protest to the Chief Constable of
Pisa, who had her tell him the whole plot and who
practically died laughing. Then he said to her, "I have
no jurisdiction over students; you should have gone to
see the President of the university. But listen here, my
dear sister, a gilt grosso is still worth quite a few soldi.
I want you to know that when I was young, we gave
girls only six soldi."

## 63
### *He wanted a young wife*

℘ MESSER Simone Spillettiera was importuned by a
friend who wanted to give him as a wife a relative of
his who was no longer young. He was saying to him,
"Now that you have completed your studies, messer
Simone, it is time that you got yourself a wife."

"You are perfectly right," replied messer Simone,
"but I do not fancy antiques."

## 64
### *The double-edged tongue of a jester*

℘ AT A gathering of learned gentlemen in the house
of Tullia d'Aragona [15] in Rome, it was said that the
poet Petrarch had cleverly availed himself of the subjects of certain ancient Provenzal and Tuscan poets and
had covered himself with honor. Some of the people
present who did not want the discussion to die out too
soon were saying that it was not true and that they
were of a different opinion. While this topic was being
argued, there came into the room Umore of Bologna;

and as he was unceremonious and forward, he immediately removed his cloak and sat down with the others. After he heard what the topic of discussion was, he was asked to give his own opinion. And he said, "Gentlemen, since Petrarch was a shrewd and ingenious person, it seems to me that he did with the verses of the ancient poets what the Spaniards do with the cloaks they steal during the night—namely, in order to avoid having the cloaks recognized and themselves punished, they adorn them with some lovely fineries and then wear them that way."

There happened to be in that gathering a Spanish gentleman who, upon hearing that his country was being rudely stung, turned to Umore and said, "What are you saying about Spaniards?"

Pretending to be stunned, Umore replied, "Oh, you are a Spaniard!"

Then he quickly called a servant, asked him to hand him his cloak, and put it back on his shoulders.

## 65
### Duke Alessandro's dog

DUKE ALESSANDRO [16] had a fine, big, fierce dog, which he loved a great deal and which he called winningly "My Love." This dog was spiteful and mean: he bit and clawed people, and he piddled on them; in short, because of these peculiarities, everyone hated him. But since he was the Duke's pet, they all put up with him.

One morning, as fate would have it, this dog died. The Duke was distressed; and when messer Berni [17] came to his palace, he said to him, "Messer Francesco, 'My Love' died. Do me the favor of writing an epitaph for him, for I want to have him buried."

Messer Berni thought for a while, and then said,
"Lord, I have it."

"Recite it to me," said the Duke; and he who was
well acquainted with the dog's temperament said,

> A dog here lies, in this dark grave;
> The meanest beast in all creation.
> He was called Love, yet was a knave,
> But had the Duke's great admiration.

## 66

### *He just dropped dead*

SEVERAL young men were seated at the table in an
inn, and they ordered some partridges. While the partridges were roasting, they ordered other things, hoping that a Florentine friend who was with them would

eat so much that when the partridges were served, he
would not be hungry. The Florentine began eating, and
the others began reciting one by one the misfortunes of
their fathers. When the partridges were brought to
the table, it was the Florentine's turn to tell about his
own father; instead he started eating the partridges
rapaciously. One of his companions asked him to tell
them what had happened to his father at the end of
his life; whereupon the Florentine came up with this
shrewd reply: "My father dropped dead."

# 67
## *It was not roasted eel*

BROTHER MARIANO DEL PIOMBO was in his day a
comical and playful man, and his pleasantries and
pranks kept the whole pontifical court in stitches. For
this reason one day a jolly gentleman decided to play
a joke on him: he invited him for lunch at his house, and
he had him eat a piece of rope in place of a piece of
roasted eel. It took Brother Mariano a great deal of
chewing before he was able to swallow it; for, as we
can imagine, the rope must have been very tough. When
he finished it, his host asked him how he had liked the
eel; and Brother Mariano replied that it was very
good, but that he had found it tougher than he would
have liked. Upon realizing that he had not been aware
of the deception, the host was even more amused in
telling him about it. Whereupon Brother Mariano retorted: "You are very wise to cook and roast ropes, for
in that way people will not be able to use them to tie
up fools like you."

## 68

### *An unhappy father*

⅌ ONE day an upright and learned contemporary of ours was asked by the Cardinal of Ravenna, with whom he was on familiar terms, whether he had any children. Since he remained silent for a while as if he were thinking of an answer, the Cardinal thought that he had not heard the question and asked it again. Finally the gentleman said, "Most Reverend Monsignor, I was on the point of telling you that I have no children, although I have three; and the reason is that I hold them in no esteem at all, and it is as if I did not have them: this is because one of them thinks he is a wise man, and instead he is the greatest fool that ever lived. The second thinks he is handsome, and he is as homely as sin; and the third wants people to believe he is courageous and bold, and instead he is more cowardly than a rabbit."

## 69

### *Witty reply of Dante to a prostitute*

⅌ DURING his exile, the Florentine poet Dante Alighieri found shelter at the courts of various Italian lords. He spent some time also at the court of Guido Novello da Polenta, who was then Lord of Ravenna; and in fact, he died there in 1321. This lord derived great pleasure from the quick and witty replies of Dante, and he often tried to give the poet the opportunity of coming up with some new ones. For, Dante, it must be remembered, was not like many of our contemporaries who try very hard to be clever and quick-witted and always repeat the same old things that would nauseate a dog—let alone sensible people.

On one occasion Guido had heard that Dante had slept with a street woman; thus, he had her come to him secretly and asked her whether Dante had been a good knight, and how many miles he had ridden. The good woman replied: "Lord, I have a poor opinion of him, and I think he is a weak man; for although he was riding a good mare, he only rode one mile."

Seeing that Dante was not old and the woman was very young, and considering that she was a prostitute and very beautiful, the Lord of Ravenna was quite surprised. For this reason he said to her, "Today I want you at all costs to make fun of him and make him blush, so be available; for we shall pass in front of your house." The woman said that she would, and when evening came Dante went for a ride through Ravenna with his lord. When the woman saw Dante riding by, she greeted him with these words: "Good evening, Mr. Ace."

Dante caught the insinuation and hit right back: "I could easily have drawn a six, but I did not like the gaming table."

## 70

### *The Tiber should not get out of bed*

A GROUP of gentlemen were discussing the damage that Rome had suffered a few days before when the Tiber had flooded the city. At one point Signor Iacopo de' Patti, a learned gentleman from Messina, who was held in high esteem for his good taste when telling pleasantries, said, "There is no doubt that the Romans should pray to God that the Tiber be sick all the time."

A man who had been participating in the conversation asked with a smile on his face as if he had heard some foolish statement: "Why, my dear Iacopo?"

He replied, "Because when it gets out of bed, it does a lot of damage."

## 71
### He had no brains

⅋ WHILE a Spaniard was trying to separate two men who were fighting he was struck on the head with a knife, and now he was having his wound dressed. As the barber was feeling his head to see whether by any chance the knife had penetrated the bone and injured his brain, messer Ortensio Albertini, who was as fine a doctor as could be found, went up to him and whispered into his ear: "How foolish can you be? Don't you realize that if he had any brains he wouldn't have interfered in the first place?"

## 72
### A rude peasant

⅋ ONE day the Archbishop of Toledo was at the window and saw a peasant who was mercilessly beating his donkey; wherefore, out of mercy for the poor animal, he began shouting from the window: "Stop! Stop, you cruel boor, before you kill him!"

Whereupon the peasant said to him, "Pardon me, sir; I did not know that my donkey had relatives at court."

## 73
### *The king knew better*

❧ A SPANIARD and a Neapolitan had come to blows near the King's palace. The Spaniard was struck across his face by such a powerful blow with a knife that one whole side of his jaw was sliced off. When he went to King Alfonso to complain about it and added that, since he was a Spaniard and furthermore he had been struck on the King's grounds, the wound had really been inflicted upon His Majesty, King Alfonso replied: "You'll find out when you bite into a biscuit!"

## 74
### *He had not completely violated*
### *Aristotle's rules*

❧ CERTAIN gentlemen were severely criticizing a tragedy, saying that it did not contain any of those requisites that Aristotle says are the principle and the goal of a tragedy—namely, the terrible and the pitiful. At one point a gentleman who was in their company said, "Gentlemen, be more careful when you criticize the literary work of another man, and do not be so hasty in passing judgment. It seems to me that this tragedy does contain one of the requisites you have mentioned." And upon being asked which requisite he had in mind, he replied: "The pitiful, for there is no man, hardhearted though he be, who upon reading it does not feel pity for the ignorance of the author!"

## 75
### A hasty judge

MESSER Girolamo Gualteruzzi was pleading his case before a judge, and at one point the judge called him a liar. Messer Girolamo said that he was telling the truth and that there was a witness who could bear him out. When, upon being put on the stand, the gentleman asserted that Messer Girolamo had told the truth, the judge turned to the latter and said, "In that case I must give you back your honor."

Messer Girolamo said, "Don't try too hard! For if you had to return the honor to all those whom you have deprived of it, you would have none left for yourself."

## 76
### Christ was among friends

A SPANIARD was in the noble city of Cosenza on the day of the celebration of Corpus Christi, and he was very indiscreetly saying that Italians were poor Christians because they never accompanied the Most Blessed Sacrament when He was taken through the city in a procession. On the other hand, he was boasting of the Spanish custom, saying that in Spain all the nobles participated in the procession. Irritated by all that boasting, a man said to him: "Brother, here He does not need a bodyguard, for He is carried among friends!"

## 77
### Bad poetry

A POETASTER who held the learned messer Anton Rinieri da Colle in high repute showed him two of his epigrams. After messer Antonio had read the epigrams, the poetaster asked him, "What do you think of them, messer Antonio? Did Catullus ever write anything like this?"

Messer Antonio replied with a sneer: "You are right, and you can be proud of it; for Catullus never wrote a single verse, let alone two whole epigrams, such as yours!"

## 78
### *He had never seen shame*

℧ SIGNOR DOMENICO RAGNIMA, an urbane gentleman from Ragusa, was kindly warning and begging a sordid friend, who was quite different from him, to refrain from an ignoble gesture which he had seen him make on various occasions, saying that thereby he dishonored and shamed his country. His friend, who was most arrogant and haughty, said to him: "Shame shame, what do you mean shame? I have never seen it!"

Thereupon, Signor Domenico replied: "What you say may be perfectly right, for shame is of such a color, although a very beautiful one, that not everybody can see it."

## 79
### *Debt can serve a purpose*

℧ WHEN messer Giuseppe Pulla, a virtuous and courteous gentleman, was asked what one could do to have people wish he were alive after he had died, he gave this shrewd reply: "Leave behind many debts!"

## 80
### *The joys of Heaven*

℣ THE EXECUTIONERS were bringing a Jew to the top
of a hill in order to hang him. The path was steep and
rugged, and two of the officers were urging him on.
One of them said to him, "You are a lucky fellow; in
an hour you will be on Abraham's bosom in the midst
of so much rejoicing, music, and song that one could
hardly wish a sweeter life; furthermore, you will find
that they have cooked for you the most wonderful
supper you have ever tasted." Thus they came to a
pass, which had a steep cliff on either side, where the
path was so narrow that only two people could go
through it abreast. Then the poor wretch, who could
not stand that chatter any longer, was seized by the ir-
resistible urge to get even with him; he pushed him
with all his might over the cliff, saying, "You go ahead
and set the table for me!"

## 81
### *A true Roman*

℣ A ROMAN courtesan who was with child was asked
whose son her child was going to be, and she replied
amiably: "Of the Roman senate and people."

# IX

## Ludovico Guicciardini
### 1521-1589

# GUICCIARDINI

LUDOVICO GUICCIARDINI was the nephew of the great historian Francesco Guicciardini. He was born in Florence, but spent more than half of his life abroad: by 1550 he had already taken up residence in Flanders, and from 1565 until his death he lived in Antwerp, where he was, for a time, in the service of the Duke of Alba.

Besides an historical work—the *Commentari* ("Commentaries"), which he may have written in the footsteps of his uncle's monumental *Storia d'Italia* (History of Italy)—he wrote *Descrizione di tutti i Paesi Bassi* ("Description of the Netherlands") and *L'hore di ricreatione* ("The Hours of Recreation"), which was published in Antwerp in 1568.

*The Hours of Recreation* is a well-balanced anthology of pleasantries, apophthegms, fables, maxims, and proverbs. By the time he made up his mind to publish his *Hours of Recreation,* his little work was already known through two editions, which had been printed without his permission and with a different title: *Detti e fatti piacevoli e gravi di diversi principi, filosofi e cortegiani* ("Jocose and Serious Sayings and Deeds of Several Princes, Philosophers, and Courtiers").

Guicciardini did not have much really new to offer: he had profited from many sources; Poggio, Castiglione, Domenichi, and also Erasmus, Bebel, and, among others, Johannes Pauli's *Schimpf und Ernst.*

Guicciardini definitely had a moral intent, and in his book he purposely avoided any statement or allusion that might be offensive to the clergy and to the Church. This, coupled with the fact that both Poggio and

Domenichi were being strongly opposed, favored the diffusion of Guicciardini's collection, which, further, was graced by an elegant and concise style. *The Hours of Recreation* met with great success; and, it was not only reprinted many times in the original Italian, but it was translated into several languages and was read by everybody. It was even used as a manual for learning Italian; and to that effect, bilingual editions were issued for English, French, and German readers.

## If only he were the King of Fools!

❧ GIULIO, a wealthy Neapolitan, had a servant who was somewhat slow-witted; and so he called him "the king of fools." As he often irritated him with that name, the servant one day lost his temper suddenly and said to him, "Would to God that I were the king of fools, for then no man on earth would have a larger empire than I; and you too, my lord, would be my vassal!"

## 2
## Donatello's revenge

❧ IN FLORENCE the Consuls of the Wool Guild were planning to have a statue made; so they called in Donatello, a famous and excellent sculptor and painter. But as he asked fifty ducats for the execution of the statue, the Consuls, who had not expected him to ask so much, became angry at him and turned the order over to a rival of his—Giovanni, who was a mediocre sculptor.

In due time, after Giovanni had sculptured the statue as well as he could, he asked for eighty ducats. Completely amazed by this, the Consuls complained to him, protesting that Donatello, who was such an excellent man, had asked no more than fifty ducats to do it. Finally, since they were unable to settle the matter satisfactorily, they referred it to Donatello himself, who immediately decreed that the Consuls should pay Giovanni seventy ducats.

When the Consuls became indignant and reminded him that he himself would have been satisfied with fifty ducats, Donatello graciously said, "It is true; and

I had reasons to be satisfied with that amount, because with my experience I would have made the statue in less than one month; but this poor man, who could hardly be my apprentice, spent over six months on it!"

### 3
### *A secret should never be shared*

℮ A MAN had buried a sum of money in a forest, and nobody knew about it except a crony of his to whom he was wont to confide all his secrets. A few days later he went to take a look at his money and found that it had been stolen. So, suspecting the truth—namely that his crony had stolen it—he went to him and said, "My business is doing better every day: I have taken in so much money that tomorrow I am going to bury another thousand ducats in the same spot as the others you know about."

His crony, who was planning to steal that sum also, returned immediately to the hiding place and put back the money he had taken; wherefore, the owner of that money went later to that place, took his money, and brought it back home cheerfully, saying to himself, "Have a crony, but beware of him!"—a saying that later became a proverb.

### 4
### *A happy cuckold*

℮ UPON returning home, a peasant chanced to find his wife in bed with a young man; as the peasant wanted to strike them on the head with an axe which he had in his hand, the valiant woman shouted at him coolly: "Don't strike us; for he is doing this for the God of

Love, and I am doing it for three bushels of wheat he
has promised me."

Fearing perhaps to offend the gods, or else pleased
with the idea of the three bushels of wheat, the peasant,
upon hearing that, turned away, and the lovers brought
their work to completion.

## 5
### *What is needed to wage a war*

WHEN KING LOUIS XII [of France] wanted to attack the Duchy of Milan, to which he laid claim, one
day, while holding a council on this, he asked Gianiacopo
da Triulzio, a most renowned and expert Milanese
captain, what preparations and provisions were necessary for such a signal enterprise. And Triulzio replied
at once to him: "We need to prepare three things, Sire
—money, money, and more money!"

# 6

## *Reply of Countess Caterina to the conspirators who were threatening to kill her children*

⁊ IN THE city of Forlì some conspirators had killed their lord, Count Girolamo, and had taken prisoner his children and his wife, Countess Caterina,[1] who was the rightful heiress. Then they seized the city; but since the castle was holding out, and the castellan refused to surrender, they felt that unless they occupied the fortress they would not have accomplished anything. Whereupon, the brave Countess thought of a most noble expedient: she promised the conspirators that if they let her enter the castle, she would make the defenders surrender; and that, as guarantee of her promise, she would leave her children as forfeits.

Having reached an agreement, the woman entered the castle and immediately went on the battlements, whence she began to rebuke the conspirators harshly for the murder of her husband and to threaten them with all sorts of reprisals. But they seized her children; and brandishing a knife, they showed that they were going to kill them under her very eyes if she did not keep her promise. Whereupon, without losing her composure, the courageous Countess quickly lifted her skirt and said to them with a fierce look, "You fools, don't you think I have the mould to make other children?" This struck them so, that, overcome with remorse for their blunder and concerned only with their safety, they let the children go unharmed and fled the city.

## 7
### *Conceit makes people blind*

℘ BENEDETTO DEGLI ALBIZI went to congratulate a
friend who had been raised to the rank of cardinal. The
Cardinal, however, whom that promotion had made
proud and pompous, pretended not to know him and
asked him who he was.

Wherefore Benedetto, who was a noble and high-
minded young man, felt hurt and changed his mind
about congratulating him. But instead, he said, "Monsignor, our friendship brings me here to condole with
you upon your fortune—or better, your blindness—
which has elevated you to this rank; because as soon
as people like you rise to similar lofty positions, their
sight becomes so dim and their other senses so dull that
they no longer know their friends or even themselves."


## 8
### *He wanted no music*
### *because his mother had died*

℘ ONE of our Florentine ambassadors left Florence
for Rome; and when he arrived, there came into his
house several musicians who, in order to earn something
as is customary, began to play animatedly. But the
ambassador, who was perhaps more avaricious than
witty, upon hearing the music, sent word to them to
stop playing because his mother had died. A little later
some gentlemen called on him; and when the opportunity arose, they asked him when his mother had died.

"Over forty years ago," the ambassador replied.

## 9
### *Reply of Pope Gregory to a flatterer*

℘ UPON hearing himself praised excessively by a certain man, Pope Gregory XIII said, "I pray God that he make me be such as you describe me and that he make such an honest man of you that your opinion will be approved by everybody."

This same Pope was once asked what was the best thing that could happen to a man; and he replied, "To die a beautiful death."

## 10
### *Witticism on the Day of Resurrection*

℘ UPON being asked when he thought that there would be the greatest confusion among men, Guglielmo Budeo,[2] who was a most learned man, replied: "On the day of the resurrection of the dead, for everyone will be looking for his limbs."

# X

## Two Wits:
## Gonnella and Barlacchia

# GONNELLA AND BARLACCHIA

PRIEST ARLOTTO was not the only natural wit about whom arose a body of anecdotes and pleasantries: he is the best known and the most popular, but there were other witty individuals whose pleasantries and jests, although by far less numerous than Arlotto's, were often repeated. It would not be an exaggeration to say that practically every important court of the Renaissance had its favorite "wit"—often a buffoon—whose purpose it was to excite the laughter of his patron and guests. But there were also other witty courtiers and buffoons who traveled from one court to another, without being at the dependence of one permanent patron. Italian collections of facetiae, as well as of novelle, provide us with the names and drolleries of many of the most popular jocose individuals: Ribi, Dolcibene, Umore, Gonnella, Barlacchia, Carafulla, Mattello, and others. But the two "characters" who, along with Arlotto, can be looked upon as the prototypes of Italian humor of the early and of the late Renaissance are Pietro Gonnella and Domenico Barlacchia. Arlotto, Gonnella, and Barlacchia represent the earthy, popular, homespun humor, which had little in common with the polite wit discussed by Castiglione.

Scholars have debated for a long time whether there were two Gonnellas—one who lived in the fourteenth century and another who flourished in the next. Today the consensus seems to be that there was only one Pietro Gonnella, who lived toward the middle of the fourteenth century: he was a shrewd Florentine who entered the service of Obizzo III d'Este, Marquis of Ferrara.

Soon a vast legend arose around him, according to which he was the author of various pranks; this is how he was portrayed by Sacchetti in several of his novelle (written before the end of the century). These and other anecdotes were repeated in the fifteenth century, and new ones were invented around Gonnella by mountebanks and writers. The whole body of these anecdotes was known as *Le buffonerie del Gonnella* ("Gonnella's Drolleries"), which circulated both in prose and in verse. In Poggio's *Liber facetiarum* there are two stories about Gonnella. Giovanni Pontano included three of Gonnella's anecdotes in his *De sermone,* and he looked upon this Florentine as a model of the witty man. After Pontano every anthology of facetiae carried a few pleasantries of the colorful buffoon: indeed, during the sixteenth century there were several reprintings of a popular volume titled *Facezie, motti, buffonerie e burle del Piovano Arlotto, del Gonnella e del Barlacchia* ("Pleasantries, Witticisms, Buffooneries, and Jests of Priest Arlotto, Gonnella, and Barlacchia").

We know very little of Domenico Barlacchi, called "Il Barlacchia." We know that he lived around the middle of the sixteenth century in Florence, that he was a town crier, and that everyone looked upon him as the town wit. After he died, someone wrote down about thirty-five pleasantries and jests that were attributed to him.

# GONNELLA [1]

## I

### *Three blind men*

ONE morning Gonnella was going to the cathedral to hear Mass. He met three blindmen who were begging one next to the other and said to them, "Take this silver coin; share it, and pray to God for me." But he did not give the coin to any one of them.

The blindmen thanked him, saying, "May God reward you for it, and we shall pray for you," for they thought he had given the coin to one of them.

As the three of them wanted to go home when the lunch hour arrived, they began saying to each other, "Let us split the coin," to which they all agreed. One of them said, "Let him who has it change it." And as each one said "I haven't got it," and each replied "You have it! No you have it," they began to hit one another with their canes.

## 2

### *All women are honest*

GONNELLA had played a trick on the Duchess [of Ferrara] and she did not like it a bit; so she decided to punish him for it. She called several of her ladies-in-waiting and told each one of them to take a good heavy stick and as soon as Gonnella came in to give him a good cudgeling and not let themselves be duped by his words. All of them said that they would do what they had been told and that they would have no sympathy for the clown.

Then the Duchess sent for Gonnella, and he came immediately; but upon seeing the clubs in the ladies' hands and realizing what it was all about, he said, "I know that you want to beat me, but first I beg a favor of you—namely that the first one to strike me be the one I have kissed most often and the one who is the greatest whore in your midst."

They all began to look at one another, saying, "I never was a whore!" Meanwhile, the clown backed away, leaped out of the room, and went on his way without receiving a single blow.

## 3
### *Women are honest to a point*

ONE day, in the Duke's presence, a group of people were talking of a noblewoman who had sold her honor. Gonnella said, "That is not surprising; there is no woman who would not do the same, and I believe that even our lady the Duchess could be had for money."

The Duke said, "If you think you can win over the Duchess, I will give you a doublet."

The clown accepted the wager; and as soon as he was able to be alone with the Duchess, he said to her softly, "Madam, there is a man who is very fond of you!" The Duchess flew into a rage and started to hurl insults at him and to threaten to have him hanged. But the clown continued: "He is the Marquis of Mantua; he is dying for your love, and you know what a handsome and courteous gentleman he is. He told me that if you let him enjoy your love, he will give you one thousand ducats; and if that is not enough, he will give you two thousand, five thousand, ten thousand . . ."

Upon hearing such lavish offerings, the Duchess said with a grin, "Keep going, and I will stop threatening you!"

Whereupon, Gonnella, beaming, ran to the Duke

and said, "My lord, bring the money; for the whore has been found." And he related the whole thing to the Duke, who later often teased the Duchess about it.

## BARLACCHIA

### I

### *Barlacchia's red doublet*

℧ ON HOLIDAYS Barlacchia used to put on a fine red doublet with matching stockings, such as town criers wear; and one morning—it was St. John's Day—he put on some brand-new clothes and went into the square. A group of friends congratulated him on his lovely new doublet, saying that it looked very well on him and that from a distance they had not recognized him. Meanwhile, they sat down; and while they were talking, a dog came up to Barlacchia, lifted his leg and wet him. When he realized what had happened, Barlacchia turned to his companions and said, "As you see, that dog did not recognize me any more than you did a while ago; he thought I was a doctor, and he came to show me his urine."

### 2

### *Why Barlacchia was refused*
### *admittance to Hell*

℧ BARLACCHIA contracted a very serious illness, and all over Florence there was a rumor that he had died. With God's grace, however, he recovered; and the first day he left the house, he went to the Medici's palace. When the Duke saw him, he said to him, "Well, are you alive Barlacchia? We had heard you were dead."

He replied, "My lord, it is true that I was in the other world, but only as far as the door; and then they sent me back as a worthless man."

The Duke asked him, "Why?"

And he went on: "I knocked, and I was asked who I was. I replied that I was Barlacchia, and they asked me what I had done in the world and whether I had left any property behind. I replied that I had not left a single thing. Then I was asked the reason for this, and I replied that it was because I had never asked for anything; whereupon they drove me away, saying that they did not want such a worthless individual. Therefore, my most illustrious lord, I beg you to give me something so that next time they will not drive me out again." That most generous Duke gave him a farm.

# XI

## *Baldassare Castiglione*

### *1478-1529*

# CASTIGLIONE

BALDASSARE CASTIGLIONE was born of a noble family at Casatico in the province of Mantua. He studied Greek and Latin with the humanists Giorgio Merula and Demetrio Calcondila, and he acquired the graces that were demanded of a cavalier and a gentleman at the court of Ludovico Sforza and Beatrice d'Este in Milan. When Sforza fell (1499), he entered the service of the Marquis Francesco Gonzaga and fought with him at the battle of Garigliano. In 1503, Castiglione visited the city of Urbino and fell in love with the elegant and cultured environment of the court of Guidubaldo da Montefeltro, Duke of that city. Thus he joined the court of the Montefeltros, and he remained at Urbino ten years. After the death of Guidubaldo, he passed to the service of his successor, Francesco Maria della Rovere. He was held in such high esteem that Guidubaldo sent him as an ambassador to the King of England and the King of France, and Francesco Maria sent him to the court of Pope Leo X in Rome.

In Rome he met many distinguished men of letters and artists and became a good friend of Raphael, who painted his portrait, which now hangs in the Louvre Museum. In 1516 he married Ippolita Torelli, who, however, died four years later. In 1520 he returned to Rome as an ambassador for the Gonzagas and remained there until 1524, when Pope Clement VII sent him to Spain as ambassador to Emperor Charles V. He remained in Spain until his death, which came to him in Toledo in February, 1529.

Besides a few poems, a pastoral eclogue, and many interesting letters, Castiglione wrote *Il Cortegiano* ("The Book of the Courtier"), which is by far his most important work. *The Book of the Courtier* was written partly in Urbino and partly in Rome, between 1508 and 1518, and was first published in Venice in 1528. Castiglione decided to write this work to honor the memory of Duke Guidubaldo and the splendor of his court. He tells us that the ladies and gentlemen of the court at Urbino used to gather in the evening in the Duchess's rooms to indulge in polite conversation and that one evening in March of 1507, upon the suggestion of Federico Fregoso, they took up a discussion of what the qualifications of a "perfect courtier" should be. Their nimble and inquisitive minds take the discussions, which are held on four successive evenings, far afield; and they discuss also the qualifications of the Lady of the Court, of a Prince, of terrestrial and Platonic love, and so on.

What is of special interest to us is that *The Book of the Courtier* gives us an excellent picture of the elegant, polite society of a typical Italian court of the Renaissance; and, further, in connection with the consideration of the desired qualifications for a perfect courtier, it presents to us an excellent analysis of wit—the various types of wit, and the appropriateness and wisdom of properly used wit in good conversation. In the process Castiglione, like Cicero in the *De oratore,* and Pontano in the *De sermone,* illustrates the various facets of wit with anecdotes, jests, and bon mots, of which only relatively few belong to the general stream of facetia tradition.

Castiglione's treatise, which is both theoretical and practical, is all the more important and interesting because it expresses the views of one of the most accomplished, learned, and authoritative gentlemen of the

Italian, indeed of the European, Renaissance. In order to illustrate the various types of wit, Castiglione recounts about eighty anecdotes and practical jokes in a most elegant and sober style. When we bear in mind the tremendous popularity *The Book of the Courtier* enjoyed in Italy and abroad, it is not surprising that Castiglione's pleasantries spread far and wide and were often retold. There is no doubt that the *Cortegiano* owes much of its lasting vitality to the balanced treatment accorded by Castiglione to the whole matter of polite humor.

Castiglione's urbanity and good taste were a much-needed antidote against the coarseness—both in style and in language—of many of the pleasantries that were being circulated in his day.

The *Cortegiano* was translated into Spanish, French, German, English, and Latin before the end of the year 1566! Since the first translation by Sir Thomas Hoby in 1561, the *Cortegiano* has been translated into English several times.

(FROM *The Book of the Courtier,*
BOOK II, CHAPTERS 41–90)

## Main Characters

FEDERICO FREGOSO (1480–1541). Nephew of Duke
Guidubaldo of Montefeltro.

FRANCESCO MARIA DELLA ROVERE (1490–1538).
Nephew of Duke Guidubaldo and his adopted heir. He
was made Prefect of Rome by the pope.

SIGNORA EMILIA PIA (died in 1528). A close friend of
the Duchess Elisabetta Gonzaga.

BERNARDO BIBBIENA (Messer Bernardo Dovizi da Bibbiena, 1470–1520). A friend of the Medici. Pope Leo X
made him cardinal.

ELISABETTA GONZAGA ("The Duchess," 1471–1526).
Wife of Duke Guidubaldo of Montefeltro.

GASPARO PALLAVICINO (1486–1511). A friend of
Castiglione.

GUIDUBALDO OF MONTEFELTRO (1472–1508).
The Duke of Urbino.

PIETRO BEMBO (1470–1547). Venetian scholar and poet.
He was made cardinal in 1539.

CESARE GONZAGA (1475–1512). A relative of the
Duchess, and cousin of Castiglione.

GIULIANO DE' MEDICI (known in Urbino as *Il Magnifico,* 1479–1516). Third son of Lorenzo de' Medici and
Clarice Orsini. At that time he was an exile from Florence.

[*Federico Fregoso is speaking*] ". . . Concerning
that which I wish in the Courtier, let it suffice to say,
besides the things already said, that he should be of
such sort as never to be at a loss to say something that
is good and well-suited to those with whom he is speaking, and that he should know how to refresh with a

certain sweetness the minds of his hearers and move them discreetly to mirth and laughter with amusing witticisms and pleasantries, so that he may give them pleasure continually without ever becoming boring or producing satiety."

. . . Then the Prefect [*Francesco Maria della Rovere*] said, laughing: ". . . be so kind as to teach us how we are to make use of pleasantries . . . and show us the art that belongs to this kind of amusing conversation that aims at exciting laughter and mirth in a fit manner, for truly it seems to me that this is very important and well suited to the Courtier."

"My lord," replied messer Federico, "pleasantries and witticisms are the gift and favor of nature rather than of art. And there is no doubt that there are some peoples who are more quick-witted than others—like the Tuscans, who are indeed very sharp. It seems that the Spaniards too are naturally witty. Yet it is true that there are many among these and other peoples who are overly loquacious to the point of becoming insipid and absurd because they do not take into consideration the kind of people with whom they are speaking, the place where they are, the occasion, the time, or the soberness and modesty which they themselves ought to exercise."

. . . [*Federico Fregoso*] "It seems to me that there are only two kinds of pleasantries: of which, one is declared in a long and continuous narrative, as we see some men do, who relate something that has happened to them or that they have seen or heard, so gracefully and pleasingly, that by the proper use of language and gestures they depict it so vividly that they make you feel that you witnessed it yourself; and this, for lack of another term, may be called *festivity* or *urbanity*. The other kind of pleasantry is very short, and consists solely of quick and sharp sayings, such as are often heard among us, or in biting ones; and unless they sting a little, they are not felicitous: these were called 'sayings' among the ancients also, and now some call them witticisms.

"So I say that in the first kind, which consists of the humorous narrative I have mentioned, there is no need of any art because nature herself creates and fashions men who have a knack for amusing anecdotes and endows them with the face, the gestures, the voice, and the words that are suited to imitate what they want. As for the other kind—namely witticisms—of what use can art be? For a pungent saying must shoot forth and hit the mark before one gets the impression that he who utters it has had time to give it any thought; otherwise it falls flat and it is no good at all. Therefore I think that it is all the work of cleverness and nature."

.    .    .    .    .    .    .    .    .

Signora Emilia said [to Bernardo Bibbiena who had just been given the task of discussing pleasantries]: "Now . . . teach us how we are to use them, how we can obtain them, and all you know about this subject. And so that we do not lose any more time, begin at once."

. . . Whereupon, turning to the Duchess and to signora Emilia, messer Bernardo said: . . . I shall say as briefly as I can what occurs to me concerning those things that provoke laughter, which is so peculiar to us that when we define man we are wont to say that he is a laughing animal. For laughter is found only among men; and it is almost always an indication of a certain hilarity felt inwardly in the mind, which is by nature drawn to pleasure and craves for relaxation and recreation; wherefore we see many things devised by men to this end, such as festivals and all sorts of spectacles. And since we love those who provide us with such recreation, the ancient rulers—Roman, Athenian,

and many others—in order to capture the good will of
the people and to feed the eyes and the mind of the
multitude, used to build large theatres and other public
edifices in which they displayed unusual sports, horse
and chariot races, combats, strange animals, comedies,
tragedies, and morris dances. Nor were such shows
shunned by grave philosophers, who often relaxed their
weary minds in sports of this kind and in banquets,
. . . and this is something all kinds of men like to
do: for not only farmers, sailors, and all those who
work hard with their hands, but also the devout clergy
and prisoners who are awaiting to be executed from
hour to hour, are constantly seeking some remedy and
medicine with which to amuse themselves. Therefore,
whatever moves to laughter cheers the spirit and gives
pleasure, and for the moment keeps one from thinking
of those irksome troubles of which our life is full.
Therefore, as you see, everyone loves laughter, and
those who provoke it at the right time and in the
proper manner deserve much praise.

．　　．　　．　　．　　．　　．　　．　　．

"Now the place and, as it were, the source from
which the laughable springs consists in a certain de-
formity; for we laugh only at those things that are
absurd and that seem to be improper and yet are not.
I do not know how to express it otherwise; but if you
reflect on it yourselves, you will see that almost always
the thing at which we are laughing is absurd, and yet
not amiss.

"Now, as far as my judgment will help me, I will
try to tell you by what means and within what bounds
the Courtier should try to excite laughter, for it is not
becoming to the Courtier to be engaged all the time
in making people laugh, nor yet in the fashion of fools,
drunken men, the inane and the inept, and especially
the buffoons. . . .

"Moreover, we must diligently consider the goal and limits of exciting laughter by derision, and who it is that we deride; for laughter is not aroused by making fun of a poor wretch or of a well-known rogue, because such individuals seem to deserve a greater punishment than being ridiculed; and the human mind does not tend to make sport of the wretched, unless they boast of their wretchedness and are proud and presumptuous. One must also be careful not to make fun of those who are dear to and loved by all and who are powerful; for at times, by deriding these persons a man could make some dangerous enemies. Therefore, it is proper to ridicule and laugh at the vices of those people who are neither so wretched as to arouse pity, nor so wicked as to seem worthy of capital punishment, nor so great that a little resentment on their part can do much harm.

". . . To go back now and declare the kinds of pleasantries that fall within our scope, I say that in my opinion there are three varieties, although messer Federico mentioned only two—namely, the urbane and amusing long narrative that aims to tell how something turned out, and the quick and witty readiness of a single phrase. However we will add a third kind called practical jokes, in which we find long narratives and short sayings, as well as some action.

"Now the first, which consist of a long narrative, are such that they are closely associated to storytelling. And here is an example: at the very time when Pope Alexander the Sixth died and Pius the Third was made Pope, your fellow Mantuan, my lady Duchess, messer Antonio Agnello—all being at Rome and in the Palace of the Vatican—happened to speak of the death of the one pope and of the creation of the other; and in discussing this with some of his friends, he said, 'Gentlemen, since the very days of Catullus, doors began to speak without a tongue and to listen without ears and thus to expose adulteries. Now, although today men are not of as much worth as they were in those days, it is possible that the doors, many of which—at least here in Rome—are made of ancient marbles, have the same powers they had then; and I am of the opinion that these two doors could clear all our doubts if we only wished to learn from them.' Whereupon all the gentlemen present were filled with curiosity and were waiting to see what was going to be the outcome of the whole affair. And then messer Antonio, who had been walking back and forth, raised his eyes as if by pure chance to one of the two doors in the hall in which they were strolling; he paused for a moment, and with his finger he pointed out to his companions the inscription above it, which bore the name of Pope Alexander, followed by a V and an I, signifying Sixth, as you know. And he said, 'As you can see this door says *"Alexander Papa VI"* [1] which means that he was elected to the papacy by the use of violence, and that he resorted more often to violence than to reason. Now let us see whether this other door can tell us something about the new pope.' And turning as if by chance to the other door, he pointed to the inscription N PP V, which meant *Nicolaus Papa Quintus,* and at once said, 'Alas, bad news; this one says *Nihil Papa Valet'* ("The Pope is worthless").

"Now you see how elegant and admirable is this kind of pleasantry and now becoming to a Courtier, whether that which is being narrated be true or fictional; because in such cases it is permissible for a man to invent without blame as much as he chooses. And in speaking the truth, he can adorn it with a little fiction —sometimes more, sometimes less, as the occasion requires. . . .

"Another thing that excites much laughter, and this too comes under the category of narratives, is the grace-

ful description of certain defects of others—lesser ones
however and not deserving of greater punishment—
such as foolish statements—sometimes simple and
sometimes coupled with a quick and biting repartee;
likewise certain extreme affectations, sometimes a big
and well-constructed lie. Just like the delightful bit
of nonsense that our friend Cesare [Gonzaga] told
a few days ago: he happened to be before the mayor
of this city when he saw a peasant come forward to
complain that a donkey had been stolen from him.
After he had spoken of his poverty and of the trick
played upon him by the thief, and in order to make his
loss all the heavier, he said, 'Sir, if you had seen my
donkey, you would realize even better how much cause
I have to grieve; for, when he had his pack on, he was
the very image of Tully [Cicero].' And one of our
friends, coming across a flock of goats led by a large
buck, stopped and said with a look of amazement:
'Look at that fine buck! He looks like a St. Paul!'

"Signor Gasparo tells of having known an old servant of Duke Ercole of Ferrara, who had offered the
Duke two young sons of his as pages; but before they
could begin to serve him, they both died. When the
Duke heard about this, he offered his sincere sympathy
to the father, saying that he was very sorry; for, although he had seen them only once, they had seemed
to him very handsome and gentle boys. The father
replied to him: 'My lord, you did not see anything; for
during the last few days they became much more handsome and virtuous than I could have ever believed, and
already they sang together like two sparrow hawks.'

"And a few days ago one of our doctors was looking
at a man who had been sentenced to be flogged about
the public square and felt sorry for him because, although his shoulders were bleeding profusely, the
poor wretch was walking very slowly as if he were

taking a stroll to while away his time; whereupon the doctor said to him: 'Step it up, poor fellow, and get out of this torture as quickly as you can.' Whereat the good man turned and stood a while looking at the doctor without speaking and then said: 'When they flog you, you can choose your own gait; this is the way I like to walk now.'

"I am sure you still remember the foolishness which the Duke [Guidubaldo of Montefeltro] told us recently about that abbot who, being present one day when Duke Federico [Guidubaldo's father] was discussing what to do with the great pile of earth that had been excavated in making the foundations of this palace, which was then being built, said: 'My lord, I have thought of an excellent place in which to put it. Have a very large pit excavated, then you can have it put into that without further difficulty.' Duke Federico replied, unable to refrain from laughing: 'And where shall we put the earth which is dug up from *that* pit?' The abbot went on: 'Have the pit dug so large as to hold both piles of earth.' Thus, although the Duke repeated many times that the larger the pit was, the more earth would be excavated, the man could never get it into his head that it could not be made large enough to hold both and kept replying: 'Have it made that much larger.' "

Then messer Pietro Bembo said: "Why don't you tell the story of your Florentine commander who was besieged in Castellina [a town in the Chianti region of Tuscany] by the Duke of Calabria? One day when some poisoned crossbow missiles that had been shot from the camp of the besiegers were found, he wrote to the Duke that if the war had to be waged in so cruel a fashion, he too would have poison placed on his cannon shot, and too bad for the side that got the worst of it!"

Messer Bernardo laughed and said: "Messer Pietro, if you do not keep quiet, I will tell all the things I myself have seen and heard about your Venetians—and there are quite a few of them—and especially when they try to go on horseback."

"Please, do not tell them," replied Pietro, "and I will not tell two other wonderful ones I know about Florentines."

Messer Bernardo said: "They must, rather, concern the Sienese, who are more prone to slip in this way; such as recently was the case with one who, upon hearing certain letters read in the Council, wherein the phrase 'the aforesaid' was used—to avoid repeating many times the name of the man spoken of—said to the one who was reading: 'Stop there a moment and tell me; is this Aforesaid a friend of our city?' "

Messer Pietro laughed and then said: "I am speaking of the Florentines, not of the Sienese."

"Speak freely, then," added signora Emilia, "and do not have too many scruples." And messer Pietro continued: "When the Florentine Signoria was waging war against the Pisans, they found at times that the many expenses had exhausted their money; and as one day in the Council they were talking of finding money for the current needs, after many ways had been proposed, one of the oldest citizens said: 'I have thought of two ways whereby we can raise quickly a large sum of money without much trouble. One of these is this: since we have no revenue greater than from the customs levied at the gates of Florence, and since we have eleven gates, let us have eleven more opened; and thus we will double our revenue. The other way is to give orders that mints be immediately opened in Pistoia and Prato, just like the one we have in Florence, and that day and night they do nothing there but mint money—nothing but gold ducats. In my opinion, this latter course is the quicker and the less costly.' "

The keen sagacity of this citizen caused much laughter; and when the laughter had subsided, signora Emilia said: "Will you bear, messer Bernardo, that messer Pietro poke so much fun at the Florentines without taking your revenge?"

Messer Bernardo replied still laughing: "I forgive him this affront because if on the one hand he has displeased me by ridiculing the Florentines, he has on the other given me pleasure by obeying you, which I also would always do."

Then messer Cesare [Gonzaga] said: "I heard a delightful blunder made by a Brescian who this year went to Venice for the Feast of the Ascension. In my presence he was telling some of his friends about the beautiful things he had seen; how much merchandise there was; and how much silverware, spices, cloth, and fabrics. Then he said that at one point the Signori went forth with great pomp to wed the sea in the Bucentaur [a ceremonial galley], on board of which were so many well-dressed gentlemen, and so much music and singing, that it seemed a paradise. And when one of his friends asked him which music he had liked best of all that which he had heard, he said: 'It was all good. But among the rest I saw a man playing on a strange trumpet, which every now and then he would thrust down his throat more than two palms' length, and then he immediately drew it out; you never saw a greater marvel!' "

Then they all laughed, understanding the foolish belief of that man, who had imagined that the player thrust down into his throat that part of the trombone that disappears by sliding into itself.

Then messer Bernardo continued: "Moreover, mediocre affectations are irritating, but when they are beyond measure they can cause much laughter—such as are sometimes heard from the mouths of certain individuals concerning greatness, courage, and nobility; or sometimes from women concerning beauty or prudery. As was the case not long ago with a lady who, during a festival, was sad and preoccupied; when she was asked what she was thinking about that made her appear so sad, she replied: 'I was thinking of something that deeply disturbs me every time it comes to my mind, nor can I get it out of my head. This is the fact that since on Judgment Day all bodies are to rise from the grave and appear naked before the tribunal of Christ, I cannot stand the anguish that comes over me when I think that my body also will have to be seen naked.' Since such affectations go beyond all bounds, they cause laughter rather than irritation.

"Now, you all are acquainted with those wonderful lies that are so well woven that they excite laughter. And that friend of ours, who keeps us well provided with them, recently told me a truly excellent one."

Then the Magnifico Giuliano [de' Medici] said, "Be it as it may, it cannot be more excellent or more ingenious than the one that the other day was given me as a certain fact by a fellow Tuscan of ours, who was a merchant in Lucca."

"Tell it to us," added the Duchess.

The Magnifico Giuliano replied, laughing: "This merchant, as he tells the story, finding himself in Poland once, decided to buy a quantity of sables, with the intention of taking them to Italy and making a large profit from them. After many negotiations, since he could not go into Muscovy himself on account of the war that was being fought between the King of Poland and the Duke of Muscovy, he, through some people of the country, arranged that on an appointed day certain Muscovite merchants should come with their sables to the frontier of Poland; and he promised to be there himself to transact the business. Thus, as the merchant of Lucca was proceeding with his companions toward Muscovy, he came to the Dnieper, which he found completely frozen over as hard as marble, and saw that the Muscovites were already on the other bank; but since on account of the war they were fearful themselves of the Poles, they came no nearer than the width of the river. They recognized one another; and after a few signals, the Muscovites began to speak in a loud voice and to tell the price they wanted for their sables. But the cold was so intense that they could not be heard; for before reaching the other bank where the merchant of Lucca and his interpreters were standing, the words froze in mid-air and remained frozen and caught in such a way that those Poles, who were experienced in this matter, decided to build a great fire in the middle of the river because, in their judgment, that was as far as the warm voice reached before it was caught by the cold and became frozen. And besides, the river was so solid that it could easily bear the fire. Wherefore, when this was done, the words, which had been frozen for a whole hour, began melting and falling with a murmur, like snow from the mountains in May. Thus the words were at once heard very clearly, although the men [from Muscovy] had already left; but since the merchant thought that those words asked too high a price for the sables, he refused to accept the offer and so returned without them."

Thereupon, everyone laughed; and messer Bernardo said, "To tell the truth, the one I wish to tell you is not so witty; just the same it is a good one, and it goes like this:

"A few days ago we were speaking of the country or World recently discovered by the Portuguese sailors

and of the various animals and other things that they
bring back to Portugal from there, and that friend of
whom I spoke to you affirmed that he had seen a monkey of a very different kind from those we are accustomed to seeing, which played chess most admirably.
And among other occasions, one day the gentleman

who had brought her back was playing chess with her
in the presence of the King of Portugal, and the monkey made such clever moves that the gentleman was
hard pressed and finally checkmated. Whereupon, being vexed, as are wont to be all those who lose at
that game, the gentleman seized the king piece—which
was very large, such as the Portuguese use—and struck
the monkey a hard blow upon the head with it; whereupon the monkey jumped out of the way complaining
loudly and seemed to ask justice of the King for the
wrong that had been done her. Then the gentleman

invited her to play another game. At first she refused
for a while by means of signs, but then she began to
play once more; and, as she had done the first time,
she again had him cornered. At last, realizing that she
was in a position to checkmate the gentleman, the monkey thought of a ruse to protect herself from being
struck again; and quietly, as if by pure chance, she put
her right hand under the gentleman's left elbow, which
was demurely resting on a taffeta pillow; and while
with her left hand she checkmated him with a pawn,
with her right hand she quickly snatched the pillow and
put it on her head as a shield against the blows. Then
she leaped before the King gleefully, as though to
acknowledge her victory. See now, whether that monkey
was wise, shrewd, and cautious."

Then messer Cesare Gonzaga said, "Undoubtedly
that monkey was a doctor among monkeys and of great
authority; and I imagine that the Republic of Indian
Monkeys sent her to Portugal to win a reputation in
a foreign country."

Thereupon everyone laughed, both at the story and
at messer Cesare's addition to the story.

Then, resuming the discussion, messer Bernardo
said, "So you have heard all that comes to my mind
concerning those pleasantries that rely on an extended
narrative and a striking conclusion. Now it is well,
therefore, to speak of those that consist of a single
saying and whose ready wit is found in a brief phrase
or in a word; and just as in the first kind of humorous
talk one must avoid in the narrative and in the mimicry
resembling buffoons and parasites and those who make
others laugh by their foolishness, so in these short sayings the Courtier must take care not to appear malicious
and bitter and not to utter witticisms and quips solely
to annoy and cut to the quick; because such men who
inflict wounds with their tongue are justly punished in
all their body.

"Among the quick pleasantries that consist of a brief saying, the keenest are those that arise from ambiguity—although they do not always induce laughter, because they are oftener praised for being clever than for being funny—as the other day our messer Annibale Paleotto said to someone who was recommending a tutor to teach grammar to his sons and who, after praising the tutor as a very learned man, said, when he came to the matter of the honorarium, that besides the money the tutor wanted a furnished room for living and sleeping, because he had no *letto* ["bed"]; whereupon, messer Annibale at once replied: 'How can he be learned if he has not letto ["read"]?' There you see how well he played upon the double meaning of the phrase *non aver letto* ["not to have a bed," or, "not to have read"]. But since these ambiguous puns are very sharp, in the sense that a man gives to those words a different meaning from that given them by everyone else, they seem (as I have said) to cause wonder rather than laughter, except when they are combined with some other kind of saying.

"Now that kind of witticism that is most used to excite laughter occurs when we expect to hear one thing and the one who replies says another; this is called 'the unexpected.' And if punning be combined with this, the witticism becomes most spicy: as when the other day they were discussing about laying a fine brick floor [*un bel mattonato*] in the Duchess's dressing room, after much talk, you, Giancristoforo, said, 'If we could take the Bishop of Potenza and have him flattened out well, he would serve the purpose very well; because to my knowledge he is the craziest man born [*il più bel matto nato*]. Everyone burst out laughing, because by dividing the word 'mattonato' ["matto nato"] you made the pun; then, saying that it would be well to flatten out a bishop and lay him as the floor of a dressing room, it was the unexpected for the listener; thus the witticism turned out most sharp and laughable."

.    .    .    .    .    .    .    .

"But among other witticisms, those are pleasingly phrased that are made by taking the very words and sense of another man's ridicule and turning them against him and giving him some of his own medicine; as did a litigant who, when his adversary said to him in the judge's presence, 'Why do you bark so?' replied at once: 'Because I am beholding a thief.'

"Another instance similar to the above was when Galeotto da Narni, on his way through Siena, stopped in the street to ask where the inn was; and a Sienese, seeing how fat he was, said, laughing: 'Other men carry their suitcase behind, but he carries his in front.' Galeotto at once replied: 'That is the safe way in the land of thieves.'

"There is still another kind that we call *bischizzi,* or "plays on words," and this is done by changing a word by either adding or omitting a letter or a syllable; as that fellow did who said, 'You must be better learned in the La*tr*in tongue than in the Greek.' And you, signora Pia [which means "pious"], had a letter addressed to you: 'To Signora Emilia *Im*pia' ["impious"].

"It is also amusing to quote one or more verses, or some other familiar saying, using them with a different purpose than the one intended by the author; sometimes with the same purpose, but changing some word. As when a gentleman, who had an ugly and disagreeable wife, replied upon being asked how he was: 'You can just imagine, when *Furiarum maxima juxta me cubat'* ["The greatest of the Furies sleeps beside me." The correct Latin quotation from Virgil's *Aeneid* is *Furiarum maxima juxta accubat* ("The greatest of the Furies lies hard by") ]. And messer Geronimo Donato, as he was going the rounds of the stations [churches] in Rome during Lent with many other gentlemen, met a company of beautiful Roman ladies; and when one of the gentlemen said,

'*Quot coelum stellas, tot habet tua Roma puellas*'
["As many stars as heaven, so many girls hath thy Rome"
Ovid, *Ars amandi,* I, 59]

he at once replied:

'*Pascua quotque haedos, tot habet tua Roma cinaedos.*'
["As many kids as the meadows, so many satyrs hath thy Rome"]

pointing to a company of young men who were coming from the other direction.

"In a similar fashion messer Marc'Antonio della Torre addressed the Bishop of Padua: 'There being a nunnery at Padua in the custody of a friar who was held to be a learned and upright man, it happened that, as the friar frequented the convent with great freedom and often confessed the nuns, five of them—namely, more than half of all of them—became pregnant; and when the thing was discovered, the friar wished to flee but did not know how. The Bishop had him seized, and he confessed at once that, being tempted by the devil, he had gotten those five nuns pregnant. The Bishop was most determined to have him severely punished; but since the man was learned, he had many friends who all tried to help him. Marc'Antonio himself went with a group of friends to the Bishop to implore some leniency for him. The Bishop refused to hear them; finally, as they kept on pleading, and recommending the culprit, urging in his excuse the opportunities of his position, the weakness of human nature, and many other things, the Bishop said, 'I refuse to do anything for him because I shall have to give an account of this to God.' And as they were insisting, the Bishop said. 'What shall I reply to God when on Judgment Day he will ask me,

"*Redde rationem villicationis tuae?*' ["Give an account of thy stewardship?"]. Then messer Marc' Antonio replied at once: '*Domine, quinque talenta tradidisti mihi; ecce alia quinque superlucratus sum*' ["Lord, thou deliveredst unto me five talents; behold I have gained beside them five talents more." Matthew, 25:20].

"Whereupon the Bishop could not keep from laughing, and greatly mitigated his anger and the punishment intended for the offender.

. . . . . . . .

"Do you not remember how wisely the Prefect replied the other day when Giovantomaso Galeotto was surprised at the fact that a man was asking two hundred ducats for a horse? For, Giovantomaso said, the horse was not worth a cent; and among other defects, it shied so at weapons that it was impossible to make it come near them. Whereupon, wishing to rebuke the man for his cowardice, the Prefect said: 'If that horse has the proclivity to run away from weapons, I am amazed that he does not ask one thousand ducats for it.'

. . . . . . . .

"Another amusing type of banter is that in which one seems to concentrate on the speaker's words instead of their meaning: . . . Messer Giacomo Sadoleto asked Beroaldo, who said that he had to go to Bologna at all costs, 'What makes it so urgent at this time that you leave Rome, where there are so many amusements, in order to go to Bologna, which is in utter turmoil?' Beroaldo replied: 'I am forced to go to Bologna on three counts,' and he had already raised three fingers of his left hand to enumerate the three reasons for his going when messer Giacomo suddenly interrupted him and said: 'These three counts that

make you go to Bologna are: first, Count Ludovico da
San Bonifacio; second, Count Ercole Rangone, and
third, Count Pepoli.' Whereupon everyone laughed because these three Counts were handsome youths who
had been Beroaldo's pupils and were then studying in
Bologna.

"This kind of witticism causes much laughter because it hinges on a reply that is different from the one
we are expecting to hear, and naturally our own error
amuses us in such matters; and when we find that our
expectation was erroneous, our mistake makes us laugh.

"But the modes of speech and the figures that are
graceful in grave and serious conversation are nearly
always becoming in pleasantries and games as well.
Note that words set in opposition add much embellish-
ment when one contrasting clause is set against another.
The way in which this is done is often very witty. Thus,
a Genoese, who was very prodigal in spending, was
rebuked by a very miserly usurer who said to him,
'When will you ever cease throwing away your riches?'
And he replied: 'When you will cease stealing other
men's.'

"And since, as we have already said, from the same
situations from which one can derive biting pleasantries,
one can derive serious words of praise as well; in either
case it is a very graceful and charming method for a
man to admit or confirm what a speaker says, but to
interpret it differently from what the speaker intends.
Just as not long ago a village priest was saying Mass
to his flock; and after he had announced the festivals
of the week, he began the general confession in the
name of the people. And as he said, 'I have sinned in
doing evil, in saying evil, in thinking evil,' and what
follows, mentioning by name all mortal sins, a friend
who was very familiar with the priest said to the by-
standers in order to make fun of him, 'Bear witness all

of you to what by his own mouth he confesses he has done, for I intend to inform the Bishop of this.'

"This same method was used by Sallaza dalla Pedrada who wished to pay a compliment to a lady with whom he was conversing. After he praised her not only for her virtue, but also for her beauty, and upon her reply that she did not deserve such praise because of her old age, he said to her, 'Madam, the only old thing about you is that you resemble the angels, who were the first and eldest creatures that God ever made.'

"Just as jocose sayings are very useful to taunt, so are serious sayings useful to praise; the same is true of well-arranged metaphors, especially if they contain a repartee and if he who replies abides by the same metaphor used by the other person. It was in this fashion that a reply was given to messer Palla de' Strozzi, who, being exiled from Florence, sent there one of his men on a certain business and said to him, with a threat in his voice, 'Tell Cosimo de' Medici for me that the hen is brooding.' The messenger conveyed the message commanded him; and Cosimo, without hesitation, replied at once: 'And you tell messer Palla for me that hens cannot brood well outside the nest' [In this case, "brood political revenge"].

"It was also with a metaphor that messer Camillo Porcaro gracefully praised signor Marc' Antonio Colonna, who, having heard that in an oration of his, messer Camillo had extolled certain Italian gentlemen who were famous as warriors, and that he had made honorable mention of him among the rest, thanked him and said, 'Messer Camillo, you have done with your friends what certain merchants sometimes do with their money when they discover that they have a counterfeit ducat: in order to get rid of it, they put it among many good ones; and in this way they pass it off. In this same fashion, in order to do me honor, although I am not worth much, you have placed me in the company of such worthy and excellent gentlemen, that through their merit I may perhaps pass as good.' . . .

"You see, then, that this situation is common to both kinds of witticism; and so there are many others, of which one could give countless examples, especially of serious sayings. Like the one uttered by the Great Captain, who, having taken his place at the table, realizing that all the places had already been taken and seeing that there remained standing two Italian gentlemen who had served very well in the war, immediately rose to his feet and asked all the others to stand and to make room for these two, saying, 'Let these gentlemen sit down to eat; for if it had not been for them, now we would not have anything to eat.' On another occasion he said to Diego Garzia, who was urging him to get away from a dangerous position that was being hit by cannon shot, 'Since God has put no fear in your heart, do not try to put any in mine.'

"And King Louis, who is the present King of France, upon being told soon after he was made King that then was the time to punish his enemies who had done him so much wrong while he was Duke of Orleans, replied that it was not up to the King of France to avenge the wrongs done to the Duke of Orleans.

"At times it is also possible to utter a biting witticism with a certain gravity, without exciting laughter. As when Djem Othman, brother of the Great Turk, being a captive in Rome, said that jousting, as we practice it in Italy, seemed to him too violent if done as a sport and not violent enough if done in earnest. And upon being told how agile and naturally athletic King Ferdinand the Younger was in running, jumping, vaulting, and the like, he said that in his country slaves indulged in these sports, but that from the time they were boys gentlemen learned liberality; and they prided themselves on it.

"Almost of the same kind, but a bit more ridiculous, is what the Archbishop of Florence said to Cardinal Alessandrino—namely that men have only their goods, their body, and their soul; their goods are put in jeopardy by lawyers, their body by physicians, and their soul by theologians."

Then Magnifico Giuliano said, "To this, one might add what Nicoletto used to say—namely that rarely does one find a lawyer who is directly involved in a lawsuit, a physician who takes medicines, or a theologian who is a good Christian."

Messer Bernardo laughed, then continued: "Of these there are countless instances uttered by great lords and very grave men. But we often laugh also at comparisons like the one our Pistoia wrote to Serafino: 'Send back the large suitcase that looks like you'; for, if you recall, Serafino looked very much like a suitcase.

"Moreover, there are some who delight in comparing men and women to horses, dogs, birds, and often to chests, stools, carts, candlesticks; which sometimes is witty, sometimes very flat; for, in this, it is necessary to take into consideration the place, the time, the people, and the other things we have mentioned so many times."

Then signor Gaspar Pallavicino said, "A pleasing comparison was the one that our friend signor Giovanni Gonzaga made between Alexander the Great and his son." "I do not know it," replied messer Bernardo. And signor Gasparo said, "Signor Giovanni was playing with three dice; and, as is his wont, he had lost many ducats and was still losing. His son, signor Alessandro, who, although still a boy, is just as fond of gambling as his father, was watching him very attentively and seemed dejected. Count Pianella, who was there present along with many other gentlemen, said, 'As you can see, my lord, signor Alessandro is unhappy with your losing and is anxiously waiting for you to win so that he can have some of your winnings. Therefore, relieve him of his anxiety; and before you lose everything, give him at least one ducat so that he too may go and gamble it with his friends.' Then signor Giovanni said, 'You are mistaken, for Alessandro is not thinking of anything as trifling as that. But, as is written that when Alexander the Great, who was then still a boy, heard that his father Philip had won a great battle and conquered a certain kingdom, began to weep; and upon being asked why he wept he replied that it was because he was afraid his father would conquer so much territory that he would leave nothing for him to conquer; in the same way now my son Alessandro is grieving and on the verge of weeping because he is afraid that I am losing so much that I shall leave nothing for him to lose.' "

After everyone had laughed for a while at this, messer Bernardo went on: "One should also avoid uttering impious witticisms; for, from that it is a short step to wishing to be witty in cursing and in trying to find novel ways of doing this . . . [and] those who wish to make a display of their wit by being irreverent to God deserve being banished from the society of every gentleman. And those persons, no less, who use obscene and foul language and who show no respect for the presence of ladies and seem to find pleasure exclusively in making them blush with shame, and who to that end are ever seeking quips and witticisms. As this year in Ferrara, at a banquet in the presence of many ladies, there were a Florentine and a Sienese who, as you know, are usually antagonistic. To taunt the Florentine, the Sienese said, 'We have married

Siena to the Emperor, and we have given him Florence
as a dowry.' He said this because there was a rumor
at the time that the Sienese had given a certain sum
of money to the Emperor and that he had taken them
under his protection. The Florentine quickly rejoined:

'Siena will first be possessed (with the French meaning, but he used the Italian word); then the dowry will
be fought over at leisure.' As you can see, the retort
was clever; but since it was made in the presence of
women, it became obscene and in poor taste."

Then signor Gaspar Pallavicino said, "That is all
women like to hear; and you wish to deprive them of
that pleasure. For my part, I have had the experience
of blushing with shame far oftener at words uttered
by women than by men." "I am not talking of those
women," said messer Bernardo, "but of virtuous women,
who deserve reverence and honor from every gentleman."

Signor Gasparo said, "We should have to invent an ingenious rule to know them, because most of the time those who seem to be the best are actually all the contrary."

Then messer Bernardo said laughing: "If it were not for the presence here of our signor Magnifico, who is everywhere alleged to be the protector of women, I should take it upon myself to answer you; but I do not wish to offend him."

At this point signora Emilia, also laughing, said, "Women have no need of a defender against an accuser of so little authority. Therefore, leave by all means signor Gasparo in this wicked opinion of his, which arises from his never having found a woman who would look at him, rather than from any failing on their part; so go on with your discussion of pleasantries."

Then messer Bernardo said, "Indeed, Madam, it seems to me that I have already indicated the various situations from which one can derive pungent witticisms, which, moreover, are the more graceful when they are accompanied by a fine narrative. Yet, one could mention many others; as when, by overstatement or understatement, one says things that are beyond credibility and verisimilitude; and of this sort was the one told by Mario da Volterra about a prelate who held himself to be so great a man that when he entered St. Peter's, he stooped to avoid bumping his head against the architrave of the portal. Again, our Magnifico here said his servant Golpino was so thin and light that one morning, in blowing on the fire to kindle it, he had been swept up by the smoke to the very top of the chimney; but he was lucky that he got caught crosswise against one of the openings, and so he did not fly away with the smoke.

"Another time, messer Agostino Bevazzano said

that a miser, who had refused to sell his wheat while the price was high, later, when he saw that the price had dropped considerably, hanged himself in despair from a rafter in his bedroom; and one of his servants, who had heard the noise, ran in, saw his master hanging, and quickly cut the rope and saved his life. As soon as the miser regained consciousness, he insisted that his servant pay him for the rope he had cut.

"To this category seems to belong also what Lorenzo de' Medici said to an insipid buffoon: 'You could not make me laugh if you tickled me.' . . .

"It is also pleasant when with a retort we reprove without apparently meaning to do so. As when the Marquis Federico of Mantua, father of our Duchess, was at the table with many gentlemen, one of whom said after eating a whole bowlful of soup: 'Pardon me, my lord,' and in saying so began swilling the broth that was left. Whereupon the Marquis said at once, 'You should ask pardon of the swine, for to me you do no offense at all.'

"Again, to censure a tyrant who was wrongly reputed to be generous, messer Niccolò Leonico said, 'Think what generosity is harbored in this man, for he gives away not only his own property, but other men's as well!'

"A very charming type of pleasantry is that which consists in a certain dissimulation, when we say one thing and tacitly we imply another. To be sure, I do not mean something completely different—like calling a dwarf a giant, or a Negro, white, or a very ugly man handsome—for these contraries are too obvious, even though at times these too excite laughter; but I mean when with a severe and grave tone we say humorously what is not in our mind. As when a gentleman told messer Agostino Foglietta an outright lie and affirmed it resolutely, since he felt that he would hardly believe

it; messer Agostino said at last, 'My dear sir, if I may
ever hope to receive a kindness from you, do me the
great favor not to mind if I never believe anything
you say.' But as the other repeated and swore that it
was the truth, he finally said, 'Since this is your wish,
I will believe it for your sake, for indeed I would do
even more than that for you.'

"Don Giovanni di Cardona said something similar
to this about a man who wanted to leave Rome: 'In
my opinion this fellow has the wrong idea, because he
is so wicked that if he stayed in Rome, in time he could
become a cardinal.' And of this sort is also what Alfonso Santa Croce said: some time before he had
suffered some abuse from the Cardinal of Pavia, and
one day, as he was strolling with some gentlemen near
the place of public execution outside of Bologna, he
saw a man who had recently been hanged. Whereupon
he turned toward the body with a thoughtful expression and said loudly, so that everyone could hear him:
'Lucky you, who do not have to deal with the Cardinal
of Pavia!'

"This sort of pleasantry that has an ironic flavor
seems very becoming to great men because it is grave
and pungent and can be used in humorous as well as
in serious matters. Hence many ancients, including some
of the most esteemed—such as Cato and Scipio Afri-
canus the Younger—have used it; but it is said that
in this genre the philosopher Socrates excelled above
all others, and in our day, King Alfonso I of Aragon.
The latter, one morning as he was about to eat, took
off many precious rings from his fingers in order not to
wet them in washing his hands and handed them to the
person who happened to be closest at hand, almost
without looking to see who he was. That servant
thought that the King had paid no attention to whom
he had given the rings and that by reason of his being

concerned with more important matters he probably
would forget the whole thing; and of this he became
more convinced when he saw that the King did not ask
for them again. When days, weeks, and months passed
and he never heard one word about them, he thought
that he was surely safe. Thus, one morning when it was
nearly a year since this had happened, and when the
King wanted to eat, the servant came up to him and
held out his hand to receive the rings; then the King,
drawing close to his ear, said to him: 'Be satisfied with
the first ones, for these will be good for someone else.'
You see how sharp, ingenious, and grave this quip was,
and how truly worthy of the magnanimity of an Alexander.

"Similar to this type, which leans toward the iron-
ical, is still another when with honest words we name
an evil thing. As the Great Captain said to a gentleman
of his who, after the battle of Cerignola, upon seeing
that there was no longer any danger, came toward him
in the richest armor one can imagine, as if armed for
battle; whereupon the Great Captain turned to Don
Ugo di Cardona and said, 'Have no more fear of the
storm, for St. Elmo has appeared'; and with these
polite words he cut the man to the quick, because, as
you know, St. Elmo always appears to the sailors after
the storm and gives token of fair weather; and thus
the Great Captain meant that the appearance of this
gentleman was a sign that all danger was passed.

"Also, once signor Ottaviano Ubaldini was in
Florence in the company of some citizens of great authority; and as they were talking about soldiers, one
of them asked him whether he knew Antonello da
Forlì, who had at that time fled from Florentine territory. Signor Ottaviano replied: 'I am not acquainted
with him, but I have often heard that he is an eager
soldier.' At which, another Florentine said, 'You see

how eager he is when he takes leave before he is given
it!'

.    .    .    .    .    .    .    .

"There are certain other sayings when a man, known
to be clever, says something that seems to proceed from
foolishness. As when the other day messer Camillo
Palleotto said of someone: 'What a fool he was! As
soon as he began to get rich, he died.'

"Similar to this kind is a certain spicy and pungent
dissimulation, where a man—a prudent man, as I have
said—pretends not to understand what he does understand, as once did the Marquis Federico of Mantua.
Being annoyed by a wearisome individual who was
complaining that some neighbors of his were snaring
doves in his dovecot, and all the while held in his hand
a dove that had been caught in a snare by one foot, for
he had found him dead that way, the Marquis replied
to him that he would look into the matter. The tiresome
fellow repeated the story of his loss not once but many
times, all the time pointing to the hanged dove; and he
would say, 'And what do you think should be done
about this thing, my lord?' At last the Marquis said,
'It seems to me that under no circumstances should that
dove be buried in the church; for, since he hanged himself, we can only believe that he was mad' [suicides
could not be buried in consecrated ground].

"Almost of the same kind was the retort made by
Scipio Nasica to Ennius. Once Scipio went to Ennius'
house to talk to him; and as he was calling him from
the street, a woman servant answered him that he
was not at home; and Scipio heard very clearly Ennius
himself tell his servant to say that he was not in, and
so he went away. Not long afterward Ennius went
to Scipio's house and likewise called him from below;
whereupon Scipio himself replied to him in a loud voice

that he was not at home. Then Ennius said, 'What do you mean? Do I not know your voice?' And Scipio replied: 'You certainly are rude; the other day I believed your maid when she said that you were not at home, and now you do not want to believe me.'

"It is also delightful when a man is stung in the same fashion in which he first stung his fellow. As when Alonso Carillo was at the Spanish court and by command of the King was cast in jail, where he was left overnight because of some trifling errors he had committed in his youth. The next day he was taken out of jail; and when he went to the palace in the morning, he entered the hall in which were many ladies and cavaliers. And as they were laughing at his imprisonment, signora Boadilla said, 'Signor Alonso, I was deeply grieved about this mishap of yours because all those who know you thought that the King was going to have you hanged.' Whereupon Alonso quickly said, 'Madam, I too was much afraid of that; just the same I was hoping that you would ask me to be your husband.' You see how pungent and clever this was; because in Spain, as also in many other localities, there is the custom that when a man is led to the gallows, if a public prostitute asks him to be her husband, he is set free.

"In a similar manner also, the painter Raphael replied to two cardinals with whom he was on friendly terms, who, to tease him, were criticizing in his presence a picture he had painted in which St. Peter and St. Paul were represented, saying that the two figures were too red in the face. Then Raphael quickly said, 'My Lords, there is no reason for amazement: I was fully aware of what I was doing, for we have good grounds to believe that St. Peter and St. Paul must be as red in heaven as you see them here, out of shame that their Church is being ruled by such men as you.'

"Also sharp are the witticisms that have in them a certain latent touch of laughter; as where a husband was bitterly lamenting and weeping over his wife who had hanged herself on a fig tree; and another man went up to him and said to him, pulling his robe: 'Brother, would you do me the very great favor of giving me a branch of that fig tree to graft upon some tree in my garden?' . . .

"We laugh also when a man has made a mistake, and, in order to mend it, says intentionally something that seems silly and yet aims at the goal he has in mind, and thereby tries to get out of it. As recently, in the Florentine Council, there were two enemies (as often happens in these republics), and one of them, who was of the Altoviti family, had fallen asleep. And although his adversary, who was of the Alamanni family, was not speaking nor had he spoken until then, in order to get a laugh, the man who sat next to Altoviti woke him up by nudging him with his elbow and said, 'Did you hear what that man said? Say something, for the Signori are asking for your opinion.' At which, Altoviti, drowsily and without stopping to think, said, 'Gentlemen, I say just the opposite of what Alamanni said.' Alamanni replied: 'But I didn't say anything!' And Altoviti at once replied: 'Of what you will say, then.'

"Similar to this is what master Serafino, your Urbino physician, said to a peasant who had received such a violent blow in one eye that it had been knocked out and who had decided to go to master Serafino to be cured. When the later saw him, although he realized that it would be impossible to cure him, in order to extract some money from him, just as the blow had extracted the eye from his head, he gave him ample reassurance that he would cure him; and so, every day, he asked him for money, promising that within five or six days he would begin to get his sight back. The poor peasant gave him what little he had. But, seeing that the cure was taking a long time, he began to complain to the doctor, saying that he did not notice any improvement; and he could see no better out of that eye than if he did not have it at all. Finally, upon realizing that he would not be able to get much more out of him, master Serafino said: 'Brother, you must resign yourself to your fate: you lost your eye, and there is no longer any remedy for it; and may God grant that you do not lose the other one also.' When the peasant heard this, he began to weep and complain loudly and said: 'Master, you have ruined me and stolen my money; I will complain to the Duke'; and he was screaming loudly. Then master Serafino flew into a rage and to clear himself said: 'You wretched peasant! So you would like to have two eyes like city folk and honest people have? Go to the devil!' And he uttered these words so angrily that the poor, frightened peasant did not say a word; he picked his way out quietly, believing himself to be in the wrong.

.     .     .     .     .     .     .     .

"We often use a word in which there is a hidden meaning that is quite different from the one we seem to intend. As did our Prefect here, when they were talking of a captain who in his time had actually lost most of his battles, but just then had had the fortune of winning one; as the speaker was saying that when said captain had entered the city in question he was wearing a very beautiful crimson velvet doublet, which he always wore after his victories, the Prefect said: 'It must be new.'

"It is also very amusing at times when we reply to something that our interlocutor has not said, or we pretend to believe he has done something he has not done, but should have done. As did Andrea Coscia who, having gone to call on a gentleman who rudely left him standing while he remained seated, said: 'Since your lordship commands me, I will sit down to obey you'; and so he sat down.

"We laugh also when someone genially accuses himself of some fault; as when the other day I told the Duke's chaplain that the Cardinal had a chaplain who said Mass faster than he, and he replied 'That is not possible,' and coming close to my ear, he said: 'I want you to know that I do not recite one third of the silent prayers.' Also, when Biagino Crivello, after a priest had been killed in Milan, asked the Duke for his benefice. The Duke had made up his mind to bestow it upon someone else; and when in the end Biagino saw that no other argument was of any avail, he said: 'Why is that? If I had the priest killed, why will you not give his benefice to me?' . . . It is also a fine and spicy way of talking, especially for grave and dignified persons, to reply in a manner that is contrary to what the person spoken to desires, but slowly and as if with a certain doubtful and hesitating consideration. As did once King Alfonso I of Aragon, who had given weapons, horses, and clothes to a servant because the latter told him that the night before he had dreamed that His highness had given him all those things; and again not long afterwards, when the same servant told him that the night before he had dreamed that he was giving him a large sum of gold florins, the King replied to him: 'From now on do not believe in dreams, for they are not true.' Of this type was the reply given by the Pope to the Bishop of Cervia who, to sound out his intentions, said to him, 'Holy Father, they say throughout Rome, and also throughout the Palace, that Your Holiness is going to make me a governor.' Then the Pope replied: 'Let them talk; for they are a lot of rascals. Have no fear; there is no truth in it.'

"Perhaps, ladies and gentlemen, I could adduce many other situations whence witticisms are derived; such

as things said with timidity, with amazement, with
threats, and with inappropriateness, or with excessive
anger; besides these, certain other singular cases that
bring about laughter when they occur; sometimes taci-
turnity coupled to a certain wonder, sometimes laughter
itself for no reason. But it seems to me that I have already said enough, for I believe that pleasantries that
consist in words do not go beyond the framework we
have discussed.

"As for those that are contingent on the outcome
of an action, although they are of various types, they
fall under a few headings. But in both kinds the main
thing is to delude the expectation and reply in a manner that the hearer does not expect; and, if the pleasantry is to be well turned, it must be seasoned with
deceit, or dissimulation, or ridicule, or censure, or
simile, or whatever other device one chooses to employ."

.     .     .     .     .     .     .     .

[*Federico Fregoso*] "In your discussion you omitted
one part that you mentioned at the beginning—namely,
*practical jokes*—and it is not right that you should
cheat the company of this. But just as you have taught
us many fine things about pleasantries and made us
bold in the use of them by the example of so many
singular wits and great men, of princes, kings, and
popes, I believe that in practical jokes also you will
give us so much boldness that we will dare to execute
some of them even on you."

Then messer Bernardo said, laughing: "You will
not be the first; but perhaps you will not succeed, because so many have already been played on me that I
am on my guard against everything—like a dog that,
once it has been scalded with hot water, is afraid of cold
water. Just the same, since you wish me to speak of this
also, I think I can dispose of it in a few words.

"It seems to me that a practical joke is nothing but

a friendly deception in things that do not offend, or that offend very little; and just as in pleasantries laughter is aroused by saying something contrary to expectation, so in practical joking it is aroused by doing something contrary to expectation. And the more discreet and clever these jokes are, the more they are pleasing and the more they are praised; for when a man plays a practical joke insolently he often gives offense, thus provoking quarrels and serious enmities. But the situations whence one can derive practical jokes are almost the same as those for pleasantries. Therefore, to avoid repetition, I shall merely say that we encounter two kinds of practical jokes—each of which might be further subdivided into various classes. The first kind is when we cleverly deceive a person in a discreet and amusing manner. The second is when we spread a net, as it were, and put out a little bait so that our man actually tricks himself. Of the first kind was the joke that a Spaniard named Castillo played recently on two great ladies, whom I do not wish to name."

Then the Duchess said, "Why do you not wish to name them?" And messer Bernardo replied: "Because I do not want them to feel hurt." The Duchess replied, laughing: "It is not unbecoming to play tricks occasionally even upon titled persons. As a matter of fact, I have heard of many being played on Duke Federico, on King Alfonso of Aragon, on Queen Isabella of Spain, and on many other great princes; and not only did they not take offense, but they rewarded the pranksters most generously." Messer Bernardo replied: "Even with this hope, I refuse to name them." "Then do as you please," said the Duchess. Whereupon, messer Bernardo continued and said:

"A few days ago there went to the court that I have in mind a peasant from Bergamo who was on business for a courtier gentleman; and he was so appropriately dressed and so smartly groomed that, although he had been trained solely to tend cattle and knew no other trade, anyone who did not hear him speak would have mistaken him for a gallant cavalier. So, when those two ladies were told that a Spanish attendant to Cardinal Borgia had arrived by the name of Castillo and that he was very clever, that he was a musician, a dancer, a ballet dancer, and the most finished courtier in all Spain, they were seized by a great desire to speak to him and immediately sent for him.

"After they received him with great ceremony, they had him sit down and began to speak to him with great respect in front of everybody; and there were few among those present who did not know that he was a cowherd from the Bergamo countryside. Therefore, when they saw that those ladies were entertaining him with so much respect and consideration, there was great laughter; all the more so, since all along the good man spoke his native Bergamasque dialect. But the gentlemen who were playing the trick had previously told those ladies that this man was, among other things, a great joker and that he spoke excellently all languages, especially rustic Lombard. For this reason they believed all the while that he was pretending; in fact, they often turned to each other with a certain surprise, and said, 'Isn't it marvelous how well he imitates that language!' In short, the conversation lasted so long that everyone's sides were aching from laughing; and he himself could not help giving so many tokens of his nobility, that in the end those ladies, albeit with great difficulty, were convinced that he was what he was.

"We see this kind of joke every day; but among the others especially amusing are those that first arouse fright, and then turn out well. For even the victim laughs at himself when he realizes that his fears were groundless. As when I was lodging at Paglia one night, and in the same inn where I was staying there were also three other guests—two from Pistoia and one from Prato—who after supper began to play cards, as people often do. Not much time had gone by when one of the two men from Pistoia, who had lost everything he had, was left without a cent; and he began to moan and to swear and curse angrily; and thus he went to bed blaspheming. After they had played for a while, the other two decided to play a joke on the one who had gone to bed. So, hearing that he was already asleep, they put out all the lights and covered the fire; then they began to talk loudly and to make all the noise they could, pretending that they were arguing over the game; and one of them said: 'You took the card from the bottom of the deck,' and the other denied it, saying, 'And you bet on a flush; it's a misdeal,' and the like, with so much din that the fellow who was asleep awoke. And hearing that those two were playing and talking as if they saw the cards, he opened his eyes a little; and seeing no light in the room, he said, 'What the devil are you doing? Are you going to shout all night?' Then he lay down again, as if to sleep. His two companions paid no attention to him and went on as before so that the man, who was wide awake, began to wonder; and seeing clearly that there was no fire or light of any kind and that yet those two continued to play and to quarrel, he said, 'How on earth can you see the cards without light?' One of the two replied: 'You must have lost your sight along with your money; can't you see that we have two candles here?' The one who was in bed lifted himself upon his arms and said somewhat angrily, 'Either I am drunk or blind, or you are lying.' The two got up and groped their way to his bed, laughing and pretending to believe that he was making fun of them; and he kept on repeating: 'I really can't see you.' Finally the two began to feign

great surprise, and one said to the other, 'Good
heavens, I think he is telling the truth; hand me that
candle, and let us see whether his eyes have grown dim.'
Then the poor fellow was convinced he had gone blind
and said weeping bitterly, 'Oh my friends, I am blind.'
And at once he began to invoke Our Lady of Loreto,
and to implore her to forgive the blasphemies and
curses he had addressed to her for having lost his
money. The two companions continued to comfort him
and said, 'It is not possible that you do not see us; this
is some fancy you have got into your head.' 'Woe is
me,' replied the other; 'this is no fancy, and I do not
see you any more than if I had never had eyes in my
head.' 'But there is nothing the matter with your eyes,'
the two replied; and one said to the other, 'See how
well he opens his eyes! And how bright they are! Who
would believe that he cannot see?' The poor fellow
kept on crying louder and louder and begging God to
have mercy on him.

"At last they said to him, 'Make a vow to go barefoot
and naked and with great devotion to the shrine of
Our Lady of Loreto, for this is the best remedy that
can be found. Meanwhile, we will go to Acquapendente
and the nearby towns to look for a doctor; and we
shall do all we can for you.' Then the poor fellow immediately knelt down on the bed. And with endless
tears and bitter repentance for his blasphemy, he made
a solemn vow to go, naked, to Our Lady of Loreto and
to offer her a pair of silver eyes, to eat no meat on
Wednesdays or eggs on Fridays, and to fast on bread
and water every Saturday in honor of Our Lady, if
she would grant him the mercy of restoring his sight.
His two friends went into another room and lighted
a candle; and roaring with laughter, they returned to
the poor fellow, who, although he was free of his great
anguish, as you can imagine, was still so stunned by

the fear he had experienced that not only was he unable to laugh, but he could not even talk; and his two companions did nothing but nettle him, saying that he was duty-bound to keep all the vows he had made because he had been granted the mercy he had asked.

"Of the other kind of practical jokes, where a man deceives himself, I shall give no other example than the one that happened to me not long ago. During the past carnival, my friend the Cardinal of San Pietro in Vincoli—who knows how much fun I get out of playing tricks on friars when I wear a mask—after he had carefully arranged beforehand what he intended to do, came one day with Monsignor of Aragon and some other cardinals to certain windows in the Banchi [an important street in Renaissance Rome] pretending that he wanted to watch the maskers go by, as is the custom in Rome. I, who was wearing a mask, came by; and seeing a friar who was standing hesitant on one side, I decided that I had found my chance, and I immediately swooped down on him like a hungry falcon on his prey. After I first asked him who he was and he answered me, I pretended to know him; and with many words I began to try to convince him that the Chief of Police was looking for him because of certain bad reports that had been made against him. I urged him to go with me to the Chancery, for there I would find a way to protect him. The friar, who was trembling with fear, did not seem to know what to do and said that he was afraid of being seized if he went far from San Celso [the name of a street and church near the Banchi]. I kept on encouraging him, however, and said so much that he mounted behind me. Then I felt that my plan had been successful; so I immediately headed for the Banchi, while my horse bucked and kicked. Imagine now what a beautiful sight it must have been to behold a friar riding behind a masker, with his cloak flying and his head tossing back and forth, looking as if he were going to fall any minute.

"At this fine spectacle those gentlemen began throwing eggs at us from the windows, and then all the people of the Banchi did the same; hail never fell from the sky with greater fury than those eggs from the windows, and most of them fell on me. Since I was masked, I did not care; and I thought that the thunderous laughter was all at the expense of the friar. For that reason I went up and down the Banchi several times under that pelting storm, although the friar kept on begging me with tears in his eyes to let him dismount, and not to shame his cloth in that fashion. But then, stealthily, the rogue had eggs given him by some lackeys stationed there for the purpose; and pretending to hold me tight so as not to fall, he crushed them on my chest, often on my head, and sometimes on my very forehead so that I was all smeared. Finally, when everyone was tired of laughing and tossing eggs, he jumped down from my horse; and pushing back his cowl, he uncovered a long shock of hair and said, 'Messer Bernardo, I am one of the grooms at San Pietro in Vincoli, and it is I who takes care of your little mule!'

"I do not know whether at that point I experienced greater grief, anger, or shame; however, as a lesser evil, I ran all the way home. And the next morning I did not dare show my face; but the laughter occasioned by this joke lasted not only through the next day, but nearly until the present."

And since the narration of this story had caused much laughter, messer Bernardo continued: "There is another very amusing way of playing a practical joke, which can be a source of pleasantries as well—it is when we pretend to believe that someone wishes to do something that he actually does not intend to do.

As one evening after supper when I was on the bridge at Lyons, jesting with Cesare Boccadello, we began to seize each other's arms as if we wished to wrestle— this, because it happened that at that time there was no one on the bridge. As we were carrying on in this fashion, two Frenchmen arrived; and on seeing our contest, they asked what it was all about and stopped to try to separate us, thinking that we were quarrelling in earnest. Then I said quickly: 'Help me, gentlemen, for at certain phases of the moon this poor man loses his mind; and now, as you can see, he is trying to throw himself off the bridge into the river.' Then those two hastily seized Cesare, as I was already doing myself, and held him very tightly; and he, telling me all the while that I was mad, tried harder than ever to free himself from their hands, while they held him all the tighter. Thus, the passersby began noticing this disturbance, and everyone ran up to the scene; and the more the good Cesare thrashed about with his hands and feet, for he was already beginning to fly into a rage, the more people came up. And because of the great efforts he was making, they firmly believed that he wanted to jump into the river; and for this reason they held him all the tighter. And so, a large crowd of men carried him bodily to the inn, all dishevelled and capless, pale with anger and shame; for nothing he said was of any avail—partly because those Frenchmen did not understand him, partly because, while I was leading them to the inn, I kept lamenting the misfortune of the poor fellow, who had thus been stricken mad.

"Now, as we have said, one could speak at length of practical jokes; but it will suffice to repeat that the situations from which they are derived are the same as in the case of pleasantries. Moreover, the examples are legion because we see them every day. Among others

there are many amusing ones in Boccaccio's tales, like
those that Bruno and Buffalmacco played upon their
friend Calandrino and on Master Simone, and many
others played by women that are truly clever and fine.
I myself remember having known in my time many
amusing men of this sort, and among others a Sicilian
student at Padua, called Ponzio, who, once seeing a
peasant with a pair of large capons, with the excuse
that he wanted to buy them, struck a bargain with him
and told him to come home with him because he would
give him breakfast in addition to the money. Thus he
led the peasant to a place where there was a bell tower
that stood away from its church so that it was possible
to walk around it; and facing one of the four sides of
the bell tower was a narrow street. When they arrived
there, Ponzio, who had already thought out what he
intended to do, said to the peasant, 'I have bet these
capons with a friend of mine who says that this tower
measures a good forty feet around, while I say that it
does not. And when I ran into you, I had just bought
this string to measure it; therefore, before we go to
my house, I wish to find out which one of us has won
the bet.' And as he said that, he took the string from
his sleeve, put one end of it into the peasant's hand
and said, 'Hand them to me.' He took the capons and
seized the other end of the string; then, as if he were
going to measure the tower, he started walking around
it. But first he had told the peasant to stay still and
hold the string against the side of the tower opposite
the side that faced the little street. When he reached
this side, he drove a nail into the wall, tied the string
to it, and leaving the man there, he quietly went off
with the capons down the little street. The peasant
stood there for a while, waiting for him to finish meas-
uring; finally, after he had said several times, 'Why
are you taking so long?' he decided to go and look, and

found that it was not Ponzio who was holding the string, but a nail driven into the wall; and that was the only payment he received for his capons.

"Ponzio played countless tricks like the above one. But there have been many other men who were amusing in like fashion, such as Gonnella, Meliolo in his day, and now Brother Mariano, our Brother Serafino here, and many whom you all know. And really, this method is praiseworthy in men who do not have another profession; but I should think that the practical jokes of the Courtier ought to be somewhat farther removed from scurrility. Further, he must beware not to let practical joking degenerate into fraud, as we see many men do, who go through the world with various wiles to get money, now pretending one thing, now another. His tricks must also not be too crude; and above all he must show respect and reverence—in this as well as in all other matters—to women, and especially where their honor might be offended."

Then signor Gasparo said, "You certainly are too partial to women, messer Bernardo. Why would you have men show more respect to women, than women to men? Should not our honor be as dear to us as theirs is to them? Is it your opinion that women should sting men with words and practical jokes in all things without any restraint, and that men should remain silent, and thank them to boot?"

Then messer Bernardo replied: "I do not say that in their pleasantries and practical jokes women should not show toward men the same respect we have already mentioned; what I do say is that they can taunt men for lack of chastity more freely than men can sting them; and this is because we ourselves have made a law, according to which a dissolute life is not a fault or a degradation in us, whereas in women it is such utter disgrace and shame that a woman who has been slandered once, regardless of whether the charge is true or false, is disgraced forever. Therefore, since in speaking of the honesty of women there is so much danger of doing them grievous offense, I say that we should sting them in some other way and abstain from this; for, if a pleasantry or practical joke stings too sharply, it goes beyond the bounds that we have already said to be proper for a gentleman."

# Notes

# NOTES

## I: Poggio Bracciolini

[1] To attend the Council of Constance, which was held between 1414 and 1418.

[2] Milanese pamphleteer, humanistically known as Antonius Luschus (1368–1441).

[3] Usually known as Can Grande della Scala. Actually Can Grande enjoyed Dante's gratitude and admiration.

[4] Eugenius IV, who was pope from 1431 to 1437.

[5] There was bad blood between Poggio and Angelotto, Cardinal of St. Mark. The latter appears, always in a bad light, in several of Poggio's stories. See, for instance, facetiae numbers 41 and 48.

[6] He had been elected pope in 1406. In 1415 he abdicated before the Council of Constance.

[7] The Western Schism, which followed the election of Urban VI, in 1378, ended with the election of Martin V in 1417.

[8] Francesco degli Azuzzoni, Archbishop.

[9] Ridolfo di Varano, Lord of Camerino, was a well-known condottiere.

[10] See note 9, above.

[11] See note 2, above.

[12] Tommaso Brancaccio, nephew of Pope John XXIII.

[13] (1361–1437) In 1433 he was crowned Emperor in Rome by Pope Eugenius IV.

[14] In the province of Pesaro, in central Italy.

[15] Eugenius IV, 1431–1437.

[16] Poggio went to England in 1418 and spent four years there.

[17] See note 5.

[18] See note 5.

[19] See note 9.

[20] See note 16.

[21] Florentine humanist (1364–1437).

[22] (1370–1378) In 1377 he brought the Holy See back to Rome from Avignon.

[23] A town in northern Italy.

[24] A great condottiere (1360–1412), who at one time was also in the service of the Visconti of Milan.

[25] A village between Florence and Arezzo.

[26] One of the early Florentine humanists (d. 1394).

## II: Ludovico Carbone

[1] (1410–1415) He was elected in Pisa against Gregory XII, so he was an illegitimate pope, and he is not recognized by the church.

[2] Borso d'Este of Ferrara.

## III: Piovano Arlotto

[1] Alfonso V of Aragon, King of Naples. He conquered Naples in 1442 and reigned until his death in 1458.

[2] Ancient Italian coin.

[3] In Florence.

[4] An inn on a hill overlooking Florence.

[5] Leonardo from Arezzo, or Leonardo Aretino, was the famous humanist and Chancellor of Florence, Leonardo Bruni.

[6] Sassetti and Dini were friends of Arlotto's. Both, it seems, held public offices in Florence in the 1440's and 1450's.

[7] Region in the Arno valley, east of Florence.

[8] A little town about twelve miles east of Florence.

[9] Rosello di Giovanni Roselli (1399–1451), a Florentine priest. He had been sent to Charles VII of France by Pope Martin V. G. Folena tends to believe that the plague mentioned in the story was that of 1450.

[10] Coins, pennies.

[11] A tiny village about five miles from Florence.

[12] The song of the cuckoo was considered to be of good omen.

## IV: Angelo Poliziano

[1] In the introduction to his edition of Poliziano's facetiae, *Angelo Polizianos Tagebuch* (Jena: 1929).

[2] In the article, "Sulla tradizione dei 'Detti piacevoli' attribuiti al Poliziano," published in *Studi di filologia italiana*, XI (1953).

[3] Grandson of the writer of novelle Franco Sacchetti.

[4] Leon Battista Alberti (1404–1472), the well-known humanist, writer, and architect.

[5] Donatello's equestrian statue of the condottiere Erasmo da Narni, called Gattamelata, is in Padua.

[6] The Ciompi, wool carders, rebelled in 1378 against the middle class.

[7] Attendolo Muzio, called *lo Sforza* (1369–1424), was a condottiere, and father (illegitimately) of Francesco Sforza. The queen mentioned in the story was Giovanna of Anjou, Queen of Naples.

[8] John XXIII, an illegitimate pope, was deposed by the Council of Constance. See facetia No. 3 of Poggio, and corresponding note.

[9] King Alfonso of Naples.

[10] Giovan Barile (Barrili) from Capua was a statesman, and friend of the poet Petrarch.

[11] He was the grandson of Cosimo de' Medici's younger brother Lorenzo, who was the founder of the later granducal line.

[12] Alfonso, son of the King of Naples Alfonso of Aragon.

[13] Wealthy Florentine merchant, who had a branch of his business establishment also in Naples.

## V: Niccolò Angèli dal Bùcine

[1] Gonfalonier of Justice. He was sent on various missions. Machiavelli mentions him in his *History of Florence*.

## VI: Giovanni Pontano

[1] Louis XI (1423–1483).

[2] (1462–1515) Son of Charles, Duke of Orléans, and of Marie de Clèves, who later became Louis XII.

[3] A Neapolitan gentleman who was a favorite of that family.

[4] The original text has *caro,* which in Latin means both "flesh" and "meat," hence the pun.

[5] Neapolitan humanist (1455–1530) and author of the much imitated pastoral novel *Arcadia.*

## VIII: Ludovico Domenichi

[1] Florence, Torrentino, 1548.

[2] "Pleasantries Collected by Messer L. D."

[3] Julius II, great patron of the arts. He was elected pope in 1503.

[4] Great condottiere (1535–1584). In the battle of Lepanto (1571) he led the papal fleet against the Turks.

[5] A Bolognese wit who appears in various facetiae.

[6] Biagio da Cesena had objected to the nudity of the figures in Michelangelo's *Last Judgment* in the Sistine Chapel.

[7] Foremost satirical poet (1497–1535) of the sixteenth century in Italy.

[8] Humanist (1398–1481) who taught in Florence, Rome and Milan. He and Poggio Bracciolini were often at odds.

[9] Venetian man of letters, remembered especially for his comedies (1508–1568).

[10] Sigismund, Emperor of the Holy Roman Empire, to whom belongs the credit of bringing about the Council of Constance (1414–1418).

[11] Tyrant of Lucca (died 1328). His romanticized life was written by Machiavelli.

[12] Ancient Italian money.

[13] Ancient Italian coin.

[14] Coin of the city of Lucca.

[15] A courtesan who had many friends among the artists and writers of the time, and a writer in her own right (1508–1556).

[16] Alessandro de' Medici became the first duke of Florence in 1530. He was stabbed to death by his cousin Lorenzino de' Medici in 1537.

[17] The poet Francesco Berni (1497–1535).

## IX: Ludovico Guicciardini

[1] Daughter of Count Galeazzo Maria Sforza of Milan, and wife of Count Girolamo Riario. When the latter was killed in 1488, she defended her rule over Forlì against the French (1494) and against Caesar Borgia (1500).

[2] Guillaume Budé (Budaeus), the great French Hellenist (1467–1540).

## X: Gonnella and Barlacchia

[1] For other facetiae in which Gonnella is the main character, see stories 12, 13, and 14 of VI: G. Pontano.

## XI: Baldassare Castiglione

[1] VI equals Sixth, but here it is wrongly read Vi (from the Latin Vis-force) with the meaning "by force."

# Bibliography

# BIBLIOGRAPHY

*(This bibliography includes only the works that were found most useful in the preparation of this anthology.)*

## ON THE FACETIA IN GENERAL

Burckhardt, Jacob, *Civilization of the Renaissance* (London: The Phaidon Press, 1944). Part II, "The Development of the Individual," pp. 93–103.

Di Francia, Letterio, *Novellistica* (2 vols.; Milan: F. Vallardi, 1924–1925). Vol. I, Chap. IV; Vol. II, Chap. VIII.

Fabris, Giovanni, "Per la storia della facezia," in *Raccolta di studi di storia e critica letteraria dedicata a Francesco Flamini* (Pisa: 1918). This, with Di Francia's detailed analysis, is a most important work.

Folena, Gianfranco, "Sulla tradizione dei 'Detti piacevoli' attribuiti al Poliziano," in *Studi di filologia italiana*, XI (1953), 431–446. A learned study that confirms, in the light of the author's studies, A. Wesselski's conviction that Poliziano was the author of a collection of pleasantries.

Gabotto, F., *L'epopea del buffone* (Bra: 1893).

Pullini, Giorgio, *Burle e facezie del Quattrocento* (Pisa: Nistri-Lischi, 1958). A thorough, penetrating study of fifteenth-century Italian jests and pleasantries.

Rossi, Vittorio, *Il Quattrocento* (Milan: F. Vallardi, 1949). Chapter IV, xiii.

## ON THE COLLECTIONS
## REPRESENTED IN THIS ANTHOLOGY

*(An asterisk has been placed before the titles of the collections from which the facetiae contained in this volume were taken.)*

## I. POGGIO BRACCIOLINI

*Facezie*. Traduzione, introduzione e note di F. Cazzamini-Mussi (Rome: Formiggini, 1927). Two other editions of Bracciolini's pleasantries have been published in Italy in recent years: one in 1924 (Milan: "Corbaccio," with an introduction by Gerolamo Lazzeri), and one in 1960 (Milan: Dall'Oglio).

*The facetiae or Jocose Tales of Poggio now first translated into English with the Latin text* (2 vols.; Paris: I. Liseux, 1879).

## II. LUDOVICO CARBONE

*Facezie di Lodovico Carbone.* Edite con prefazione da Adb-El-Kader Salza (Livorno: Raffaello Giusti, 1900).

## III. PIOVANO ARLOTTO (ARLOTTO MAINARDI)

*Motti e facezie del Piovano Arlotto.* A cura di Gianfranco Folena (Milan-Naples: Riccardo Ricciardi, 1953). A critical edition, and by far the best and most accurately documented. It contains many illustrative notes, a critical apparatus, and a glossary.

*Die Schwänke und Schnurren des Pfarrers Arlotto,* gessamelt und herausgegeben von Albert Wesselski (2 vols.; Berlin: A. Duncker, 1910). An excellent edition with ample notes.

## IV. ANGELO POLIZIANO

*Angelo Polizianos Tagebuch* (1477–1479). Mit vierhundert Schwänken und Schnurren aus den Tagen Lorenzos des Grossmächtigen und seiner Vorfahren. Zum ersten Male herausgegeben von Albert Wesselski (Jena: 1929). The only complete edition available to date. A scholarly edition, with a masterful study of the history of the collection. Each item is first given in the original Italian, and then translated into German. Almost every item is illustrated with abundant notes.

## V. NICCOLÒ ANGÈLI DAL BÙCINE

*Facezie e motti dei secoli XV e XVI.* Codice inedito Magliabechiano (Bologna: Romagnoli, 1874). With an introduction by G. Papanti.

## VI. GIOVANNI PONTANO

*De sermone libri sex.* Ediderunt S. Lupi et A. Risicato (Lucani: in Aedibus Thesauri Mundi, 1954).

## VII. LEONARDO DA VINCI

*Le facezie.* In *Frammenti letterari e filosofici,* trascelti da Edmondo Solmi (Florence: Barbera, 1925).

## VIII. LUDOVICO DOMENICHI

*Facetie, motti et burle di diversi signori et persone private.* Raccolte per M. Lodovico Domenichi et da lui di nuovo del settimo libro ampliate (Venice: F. B. Bonfadino, 1609). One of the numerous editions that were made through the centuries of Domenichi's large collection.

*Facezie.* A cura di Giovanni Fabris (Rome: Formiggini, 1923). This edition offers a selection of 455 facetiae.

## IX. LUDOVICO GUICCIARDINI

*Ore di ricreazione.* A cura di Giovanni Fabris (Rome: Formiggini, 1924).

## X. GONNELLA AND BARLACCHIA

*Facezie, motti, buffonerie et burle del Piovano Arlotto, del Gonella et del Barlacchia* (Florence: Giunti, 1565).

## XI. BALDASSARE CASTIGLIONE

*Il libro del Cortegiano.* A cura di Vittorio Cian (Florence: Sansoni, 1947). Of this work there are several English translations; the most readily available is the one by Charles S. Singleton (New York: Doubleday, 1929).